THE EUROPEAN HISTORY SERIES
SERIES EDITOR
KEITH EUBANK

ARTHUR S. LINK
GENERAL EDITOR FOR HISTORY

THE EUROPEAN

HOME FRONTS

1939–1945

EARL R. BECK

PROFESSOR EMERITUS

FLORIDA STATE UNIVERSITY

HARLAN DAVIDSON, INC.

ARLINGTON HEIGHTS, ILLINOIS 60004

Library of Congress Cataloging-in-Publication Data

Beck, Earl R. (Earl Ray), 1916–
    The European home fronts, 1939–1945 / Earl R. Beck.
        p. cm.—(The European history series)
    Includes bibliographical references and index.
    ISBN 0-88295-906-9
    1. World War, 1939–1945—Europe.   2. Europe—History—1918–1945.
I. Title.   II. Series: European history series (Arlington Heights, Ill.)
D744.B44   1993
940.53′4—dc20   92-42185
                                                                            CIP

Cover illustration: Hungry child with food bucket, Holland, 1944. Photograph
by Emmy Andriesse, courtesy Leyden University Printroom, The Netherlands.

Manufactured in the United States of America
97   96   95   94   93   1   2   3   4   5   MG

FOREWORD

Now more than ever there is a need for books dealing with significant themes in European history, books offering fresh interpretations of events which continue to affect Europe and the world. The end of the Cold War has changed Europe, and to understand the changes, a knowledge of European history is vital. Although there is no shortage of newspaper stories and television reports about politics and life in Europe today, there is a need for interpretation of these developments as well as background information that neither television nor newspapers can provide. At the same time, scholarly interpretations of European history itself are changing.

A guide to understanding Europe begins with knowledge of its history. To understand European history is also to better understand much of the American past because many of America's deepest roots are in Europe. And in these days of increasingly global economic activity, more American men and women journey to Europe for business as well as personal travel. In both respects, knowledge of European history can deepen one's understanding, experience, and effectiveness.

The European History Series introduces readers to the excitement of European history through concise books about the great events, issues, and personalities of Europe's past. Here are accounts of the powerful political and religious movements which shaped European life in the past and which have influenced events in Europe today. Colorful stories of rogues and heroines, tyrants, rebels, fanatics, generals, statesmen, kings, queens, emperors, and ordinary people are contained in these concise studies of major themes and problems in European history.

Each volume in the series examines an issue, event, or era which posed a problem of interpretation for historians. The chosen topics are neither obscure nor narrow. These books are neither historiographical essays, nor substitutes for textbooks, nor monographs with endless numbers of footnotes. Much thought and care have been given to their writing style to avoid academic jargon and overspecialized focus. Authors of the European History Series have been selected not only for their recognized scholarship but also for their ability to write for the general reader. Using primary and secondary sources in their writing, these authors bring alive the great moments in European history rather than simply cram factual material into the pages of their books. The authors combine more in-depth interpretation than is found in the usual survey accounts with synthesis of the finest scholarly works, but, above all, they seek to write absorbing historical narrative.

Each volume contains a bibliographical essay which introduces readers to the most significant works dealing with their subject. These are works that are generally available in American public and college libraries. It is hoped that the bibliographical essays will enable readers to follow their interests in further reading about particular pieces of the fascinating European past described in this series.

Keith Eubank
Series Editor

CONTENTS

INTRODUCTION

Warfare has always created trauma for civilians as well as for the soldiers who fight the battles. Pillage, rape, slavery, famines, and epidemics all have been the dark companions of glorious deeds on the battlefields. But civilians, unlike soldiers, do not normally win medals for bravery in the face of these trials.

World War II brought an accentuation of the hardships faced by both soldiers and civilians. Part of this change was due to the unparalleled size and scope of the conflict—the number of nations involved, the millions of combatants, and the destructiveness of the weapons employed. But the magnitude of the warfare itself was in part the product of totalitarian regimes, governments which asserted the principle that all citizens were a part of one, all-encompassing unity, that society was a kind of gigantic machine manipulated from above in which all those below the leadership group were mere cogs. As a consequence World War II became known as a "total war" set apart from all previous human conflict. Before it ended, the regimes that were not totalitarian had also become so deeply involved that all their citizens, although never manipulated as ruthlessly as those under fascism or communism, were as much a part of the conflict as the subjects they were fighting against.

The totalitarian countries enforced the compliance of their citizens by a combination of propaganda and police action. Huge state bureaucracies provided official views of the progress of the war and then assessed the degree to which these reports were accepted by their citizens. Democratic regimes also provided official information but allowed their citizens to criticize and to gossip about war events without fear of police action. In the long run, however, all nations found that encouraging voluntary compliance with war goals produced better results than relying on force and fear.

Being on the home front in the United States was a far differ-ent experience than it was in Europe. For Americans in World War II the home front was distant from the field of battle. It is true that those at home suffered the ineffable pain of concern for husbands, sons, and friends locked in the horrible struggle against the Japanese in the Pacific. They endured the slow train-ing of men and the transfer of units to Britain for the coming battle against Germany's "Fortress Europe." They learned of the first direct involvement of Americans in the air combat over Eu-rope and heard the sagas (often misleading) of the achievements of American "Flying Fortresses." Women at home moved in in-creasing numbers into defense industries. Many goods once available in abundance became difficult to obtain. New tires were scarcely available—even recaps required a permit for pur-chase. Gasoline and many foods were rationed. Drives to raise money for defense and scrap collections for various items were common events. But the war itself was still "over there" as it had been in World War I.

In Europe the home front was often also a battle front. Only in England was there something of the same sense of being re-moved from combat that the United States experienced. Even there, however, regular aerial bombings shattered the quiet of the homeland. Elsewhere the war brought actual fighting into the territory of the homeland—France was invaded early and late in the war; Germany experienced four years of bombing and complete regimentation of its home territory; the Soviet Union endured four years of ceaseless conflict at home until Red Army troops freed areas occupied and ravaged by the enemy. And the smaller countries from Norway and Finland in the north to Italy and the Balkan countries in the south found their home soil overrun by the military forces of larger, more aggressive neigh-bors.

In Europe, therefore, there was never the detachment from violence that Americans enjoyed. The hardships and suffering of Europeans place their home front memories of World War II in a very different framework from that of Americans. Those memories, those experiences, have survived the wartime genera-tion. Even today as the Cold War declines, these recollections generate reactions that influence the course of current events.

This brief summary of those wartime experiences may serve to provide Americans with a fuller understanding of the dynamic changes taking place in Europe today.

Naturally, it is impossible to discuss the fate of every European country in a study of this size. The neutral countries of Sweden and Switzerland are not included, although their homelands might have become home fronts if the Germans had won. As it was, they provided havens for some Jews and political opponents of the Germans. Spain and Portugal, although both basically fascist regimes, also remained neutral. The roles of Rumania, Hungary, Albania, and Bulgaria, all of which had some involvement in the fighting, have not been described here. The final verdict on their activities has yet to be written.

1 / GREAT BRITAIN:
THE ISLANDS FORTRESS

In no country involved in World War II were the civilians more a part of the nation's war effort than they were in Great Britain. It was a long war for them. During the six-year period from September 3, 1939, to final surrender of the Japanese on September 2, 1945, the British public experienced the pangs of defeat, the dangers of invasion, the trauma of relentless bombing, the hardships of wartime rationing, and the strain of total commitment to the production of weapons and munitions. That Britain emerged from the war as one of the major architects of the final victory reflected the moral strength of the people, civilians as well as those in the armed forces.

THE APPEASEMENT ERA

World War II was a war that no one in Great Britain wanted. Twenty years earlier World War I had left Britain much weakened by four years of desperate fighting. The horrors of that experience had engendered a significant pacifist movement and strengthened the Labour Party's criticisms of the management of British industry and mining. This in turn added to the fears of conservative Englishmen, who worried about the spreading influence of communism sparked by sympathizers with the Bolshevik Revolution in Russia. Mussolini's fascist "solution" for controlling labor movements and leftists found considerable sympathy in Great Britain. By the time Adolf Hitler came to power in Germany, there was little inclination on the part of Britain's leaders to object to another regime that was so staunchly anticommunist. The efforts to appease Hitler and avoid war lasted until the very day German forces marched into Poland.

It is easy in retrospect to condemn Britain's leaders and many of its citizens for this seemingly timorous effort to appease Hitler. The movies taken by newsmen of the German military demonstrations should have convinced them of the impossibility of negotiating any reasonable settlement. But the harsh memories of thousands of British soldiers dying in the trenches of France a generation ago were still vivid. Thousands more had returned home wounded mentally or physically. The monetary costs of World War I had left Britain wounded economically. And a new war portended not only fresh battle losses and tremendous costs, but the dread of large-scale civilian deaths from the skies. Seemingly, there was no real defense against potential bombing attacks. The phrase "the bombers will always get through" suggested that in a future war the English channel would no longer provide real security for the homeland.

Americans should be more sympathetic with appeasement than they have been. In the United States the 1930s was the era of isolationism, of the determination that never again should American boys be sent to die overseas. American revulsion at the rise of Hitler and the Nazi regime was matched by an equal revulsion for the harsh dictatorship on the left, the Communist regime in the Soviet Union. Undoubtedly there was a significant public feeling that perhaps Hitler might blunt the spread of Communism. And many Americans clung to this feeling well into the war period itself.

Neville Chamberlain was a particularly tragic figure during this period. As Britain's prime minister he had walked the second mile in his efforts to avoid war. His efforts to negotiate with Hitler failed because he assumed that the Führer was a reasonable, sincere, and conscientious man like himself seeking to reach a mutually satisfactory deal; only too late did he discover that Hitler regarded deception as a perfectly acceptable means of statecraft. The western efforts to alleviate Hitler's "concern" for the welfare of the ethnic Germans assigned after World War I to the mostly Slavic state of Czechoslovakia resulted in the Munich Conference and ultimately in the loss by that state of its strategic defense system on its frontiers with Germany. Not only did Britain desert a democratic state at the Munich Conference, but it pressured the Czechs to accept this agreement as though it were doing them a favor. Within six months time, Germany extended its control over all of Czechoslovakia.

This, in turn, was followed by German pressure on Poland. Through much of the interim period between the wars, Poland had been under the military dictatorship of war hero Marshal Josef Pilsudski and later, after his death, of military leaders associated with the marshal. With Hitler's intentions now clear, neither Chamberlain nor Britain's French allies could afford further appeasement. Nevertheless, Chamberlain could not easily turn to Joseph Stalin to help guarantee Polish security, for the Soviet Union still claimed a third of Poland's eastern territory that had been given to that new country after World War I. Consequently Great Britain and France could only offer a meaningless guarantee of Poland's independence without any means of implementing it except a declaration of war on Germany. This came on September 3, 1939.

Chamberlain remained prime minister as Britain reluctantly accepted the inevitable. Although he strengthened his cabinet by placing it on a war footing (he included one of his major critics, Winston Churchill, as First Lord of the Admiralty and a member of the War Cabinet), the Labour and Liberal parties still remained in opposition. And the public found little ground for optimism in the initial events of the war.

It is ironic that the strategy of Blitzkrieg had been anticipated by a British military expert, General J. F. C. Fuller. He had been a prophet without an audience in his homeland and in France. Consequently, neither Britain nor France was able to provide effective aid against the Blitzkrieg Germany launched against Poland. And a week before the invasion, the Soviet Union shocked the British and the French by not only refusing to aid the Poles, but also by signing a non-aggression pact with Germany that enabled Hitler to carry out his attack.

The British public, as well as their American counterparts overseas, watched with a deep sense of shock as German armed forces divided and slaughtered the outmatched Polish army. They listened (as did the author) to the daily radio broadcasts from beleaguered Warsaw, preceded by the notes of the Polish national anthem that signalled that the city was still holding out against its attackers. But the severe bombardment of the city from the air, as well as of smaller cities and towns, even villages, took its toll. On September 27, 1939, Warsaw fell. Some Polish troops escaped the German juggernaut and fought with the French and British in the west. Other Poles followed long and circuitous routes from German and Polish territories to Great Britain. Polish intelligence sources were to furnish the Enigma machines that allowed Britain to decode German military messages and later provided information on the German development of the V-weapons. But Britain was not to be very hospitable to Polish refugees, who still quarreled over problems of leadership. The most significant contribution of Polish troops serving with British forces came in the Italian campaign, where they earned high praise for courage in battle.

After the defeat of Poland there was a hiatus on the battle front. Fear of attacks on the British supply lines grew as German submarines began threatening merchant ships. On October 14, 1939, a German submarine entered the British naval staging area at Scapa Flow and sank the British battleship H.M.S. *Royal Oak*, shocking the British public. German air attacks also threatened British naval forces. But as postwar research has indicated, Germany had far fewer submarines in 1939 than Britain had estimated. The later years of the war were to record much more serious damage to British shipping.

The period between the defeat of Poland and the opening of the German attack on France on May 10, 1940, has been labeled the "Phony War" or the Sitzkrieg (in contrast to the Blitzkrieg). During these months Britain sent ten divisions to join the French in protecting their frontiers. Perhaps it might have done more. By December 31, 1939, Britain had a million-and-a-half men in military service along with 43,000 women. But most of these recruits would require military training before they could be employed in battle, and British strategists in the early months of the war thought more of using these troops in the Scandinavian theater than in France. British troops were "going to hang out their washing on the Siegfried Line" while the Germans played popular phonograph records for their enemies, seeking to convince them that they had no hostile intentions.

Britain's largest immediate concern was to fend off a potential bombing of the homeland by the German air force. The size and capabilities of the Luftwaffe had been much overestimated. In the diplomatic negotiations that had preceded the war there had been a presumption that the bombers would easily overmatch any air raid defenses. Consequently, in the early days of the war three-and-a-half million people were moved to remote areas considered safer from the anticipated bombings. For many of these evacuees and for their hosts in their new locations, there were enormous problems. Millions of poorer people in "modern" Britain had no acquaintance with toilet facilities, had never used toothbrushes or toothpaste, had never worn pajamas. They sometimes carried on their persons lice and scabies, which horrified their host families. In spite of efforts to promote cooperation between parties, many evacuees returned to their familiar but more dangerous home cities. More evacuations followed later. And a totally different kind of "evacuation" occurred as some two million of Britain's wealthier citizens moved to safer areas. Many of them sent their children to the United States. The letters sent to these children and friends from those who remained at home provided Americans with personal accounts of the German raids.

In the early days of the war there was much digging—in parks in the big cities, in the back yards of homes, and along the coasts. In spite of the likelihood of war, little had been done to provide public air raid shelters. Britain never created the extensive and sophisticated public shelters found in Germany, nor did it shore up its existing fire fighting equipment as their enemies had. With the outbreak of war the government began to provide primitive but fairly effective family shelters that could be set up by householders in their gardens. These "Anderson shelters," named after Sir John Anderson, the Home Secretary at the outbreak of war, were made of corrugated steel sections that were supposed to be bolted together and buried. In spite of the difficulties concerned, many civilians managed to properly assemble and bury the shelters, which did offer some protection from blasts other than direct hits. But in the British rains they frequently flooded, and pumping out the water became a repetitive exercise throughout the war years.

Wealthier Londoners and residents of other endangered cities often chose a room in their homes for bulwarking against the bombing. Although these precautions provided more convenient and in some cases more secure protection than the Anderson shelters, direct bomb hits often resulted in the entombment of the occupants.

The potential use of poison gas caused great alarm in Britain. Gas masks were distributed and had to be carried everywhere one went. Smaller "Mickey Mouse" masks with red rubber face pieces and bright eye rims were handed out to children. And the skies above the larger cities and along the beaches darkened with the drab shapes of the barrage balloons suspended on rows of cables; they were designed to discourage strafing.

CHURCHILL BECOMES BRITAIN'S WAR LEADER

It was remarkable that Neville Chamberlain survived the failure of his appeasement policy as long as he did. It was, perhaps, even more remarkable that the man who replaced him on May 10, 1940, shared in the responsibility for the failed British campaign in Norway a month earlier that had toppled the government. Winston Churchill had brought dynamism to Chamberlain's War Cabinet. He had directed the beginnings of antisubmarine action and the efforts to destroy German sea raiders on British commerce, a strategy which had resulted in the destruction of the German pocket battleship, *Graf Spee*. He had unsuccessfully sought to launch magnetic mines into German ports on the Baltic and in the mouth of the Rhine. (French fear of German retaliation had prevented this scheme from succeeding.) Churchill was the strongest advocate of a British strike to shut off the flow of Swedish iron ore to Germany through Norwegian seaports. In his memoirs Churchill blamed others for the delays and the mismanagement of the efforts to invest the Norwegian seaports at Narvik and Trondheim, but certainly he was not completely free of responsibility for the failure of these expeditions that resulted in the Nazi conquest of Denmark and Norway.

It was, therefore, somewhat surprising that he emerged as Britain's wartime leader. As Chamberlain prepared to step down as Prime Minister, the two most likely choices for his replacement were Churchill and Lord Halifax, who was, perhaps, less tainted by the Norwegian fiasco. But Halifax himself doubted his ability to lead the nation since he was not a member of the House of Commons. Events proved him correct. After being named Prime Minister, Churchill was able to bring into his wartime cabinet Clement Attlee, A. V. Alexander, and Arthur Greenwood of the Labour Party and Sir Archibald Sinclair of the Liberal Party. He later would add such dynamic Labour leaders as Herbert Morrison, Ernest Bevin, Hugh Dalton, and Sir Stafford Cripps.

These and other able leaders from all three British parties contributed to the direction of the war effort. But it was Churchill who dominated the action. It is difficult in retrospect to imagine anyone other than Churchill as the leader of wartime Britain. From the very day he assumed office Churchill was coining the words that captured popular imagination:

> I have nothing to offer but blood, toil, tears and sweat. You ask, What is our policy? I will say: It is to wage war, by sea, land, and air, with all our might and with all the strength that God can give us. [And, he added,] What is our aim? I can answer in one word: victory, victory at all costs, victory in spite of all terror; victory, however long and hard the road may be.

At times Churchill's government approached the character of a one-man dictatorship, but his approval rating never sank below 78 percent, and he saw to it that the framework of parliamentary government always remained in place. Churchill's speeches, carefully crafted and personally prepared in six-to-eight-hour sessions, provided for the public the combination of lofty self-confidence and national pride that made the pudgy little man with the cigar the very symbol of every British citizen's determination to survive and win the victory.

It is, perhaps, difficult for someone who did not live through World War II to appreciate the leadership displayed by both Churchill and Franklin D. Roosevelt in maintaining public morale during those years of travail. Both men exhibited a mastery of language and a bold self-confidence that comforted and cheered the citizens of both nations. Both used the radio and the newsreel in a skillful way that even experienced political leaders on the Continent could not duplicate. Moreover, both men had early recognized the dangers associated with the Nazi regime. When Churchill came to power he immediately sought to add urgency to Roosevelt's existing concern for the German threat to Great Britain. He played rather artfully upon the common links that joined him—the former head of the British Admiralty—and Roosevelt, who had been Assistant Secretary of the Navy in World War I. Churchill also had clear indications that Roosevelt, although prevented from assisting Britain outright by the strength of American isolationism, was strongly sympathetic to Churchill's cause. Still, American aid to the British came very slowly.

By the time Churchill took office much had been done to gird Britain for war. At the end of 1939 a million-and-a-half men were enrolled in military service. Trenches had been dug in some parks. The barrage balloons had been raised over major cities to protect against air raids. Controls had been established over imports and their distribution. Nine-tenths of the principal imported raw materials became the exclusive property of state monopolies. In the years that followed an enormous extension of these measures occurred.

Churchill's assumption of office was quickly followed by Germany's sweep through France and the dramatic evacuation from Dunkirk. The participation of hundreds of British citizens who crossed the channel to assist in gathering up trapped British soldiers at Dunkirk was an early sign of the bulldog determination with which Britain would fight the war. Although 200,000 British troops were returned home in this operation, they left behind sizeable quantities of guns, tanks, and heavy equipment. Four hundred and seventy-four planes had also been lost in the efforts to protect the evacuation. The German forces moved on to humble the French and accept a surrender from a compliant government.

Britain was now left alone to confront the Germans and their Italian allies. It faced the serious possibility of invasion from a foe that now controlled the whole western coastline of Europe. Dunkirk was followed by a relatively calm period during which some British civilians still walked in the parks in the evening. Meanwhile the army continued its rapid mobilization, adding more than a million men before the end of 1940, including more than half of British males between the ages of twenty and twenty-five, one-fifth of the entire male population between sixteen and forty. Soldiers assigned to guard the coasts and members of the Local Defence Volunteers, a kind of local militia, found their efforts hampered by a serious shortage of arms. At the outset about all they could accomplish was to pull down the existing road signs so that potential intruders could not find their way around; they also scattered old cars and other debris across roads to obstruct the movement of enemy motorized units. Eventually help came from the United States in the form of a half-million rifles, but these arms came packed in grease and proved difficult for amateurs to clean. The Local Defence Volunteers, later redesignated the "Home Guard," enrolled so many in its ranks that World War II became known simply as "the People's War."

THE BATTLE OF BRITAIN

Hitler did indeed plan to invade the British Isles. But in spite of the damage wreaked by German submarines, the German navy, after losses in the Norwegian campaign, was in no condition to challenge British naval defenses. Hitler thus accepted the assurance of his air marshal, Hermann Göring, that he could take control of the skies over the channel and clear the way for possible landings that would be made by the motley collection of vessels which Hitler began to accumulate in the French and Dutch channel seaports.

In the early days of the Battle of Britain, civilians were chiefly observers. The Luftwaffe carried out its attacks principally on British military aircraft fields and planes. Although the British R.A.F. was at the outset numerically inferior to the German Luftwaffe, Britain's factories were working full tilt at producing new planes, and their levels of production were higher than those of the Germans. Britain used radar (the word was coined in 1943) to great advantage in targeting incoming planes. Furthermore, the German bombers employed were far inferior to those later employed by the British and Americans. The German Messerschmitt 109 fighter was excellent, but its range was too short to provide adequate defense for the bombers. British Spitfires frequently engaged the Me. 109s in dogfights, while the slower Hurricanes took a heavy toll on the bombers. The British aircraft industry, operating at record capacity, produced over 1,500 fighters in the four months from April through July 1940. In addition British planes shot down over the homeland could sometimes be repaired, while German planes lost in the melee could not be recovered.

In retrospect, military experts have suggested that if the Germans had continued to target the airfields, the results might have been catastrophic for the British. The toll on British pilots and the potential destruction of radar installations would have been more critical than the loss of planes. Britain lost 222 fighter pilots in this early period, with an additional 205 wounded. It took eleven months to train new pilots and partially trained pilots were far more likely to become casualties. By concentrating on airfield and radar installations Göring might have made his threats come true. But the Germans overestimated the amount of damage done and moved on to their next objective. Although it has been long asserted that the initial attack on civilian areas of London was accidental, there are also indications that the Germans intended the raid as a preliminary step to Operation Sea Lion, the invasion of Britain.

The days of the so-called Blitz on London followed from September 1940 to May 1941. London was a suitable target because of its sizeable shipping facilities, and its location on the Thames River and near the Atlantic Ocean made it an easy mark for night missions (as Hamburg was later to be for British attacks). In comparison with some of the British raids on Germany later in the war, those of the Blitz were relatively small. Early raids were carried out by an average of 160 German bombers. The numbers grew to 410 on October 15 and 449 on November 14, when the Germans bombed Coventry. Throughout the period which followed, until the German invasion of the Soviet Union in June 1941, the Germans were able to gather together from 350 to 500 bombers for their frequent sorties over the island. The size of the bombs increased during the later raids. The largest were the parachute bombs weighing two-and-a-half tons, a foreshadowing of the later Allied "blockbusters." Accompanying these were the thermite incendiaries, eighteen-inch-long bottles, packed seventy-two to the average "bread basket" and sometimes equipped with explosives to make them more dangerous to extinguish. In the wake of many raids unexploded bombs were left behind. They had to be found, uncovered, and defused by demolition squads. This operation required nerves of steel, and even then many lost their lives trying to extinguish these live "duds."

The eastern sectors of London suffered grievously due to their proximity to harbor facilities, armament works and other industrial factories, and storage facilities for goods brought in from overseas. The area was heavily populated by working-class groups, often poorly paid and poorly housed. As a consequence, fires started in this area ravaged large sections that were insufficiently equipped with air raid shelters and fire-fighting equipment. As the attacks continued, some 1.4 million people were rendered homeless.

Public air raid shelters were grossly inadequate and conditions in them often deplorable. Observers who entered them could see criminals and prostitutes plying their trades and might retreat with disgust from the collective stench of foul air emanating from the unwashed bodies. As the raids continued, the subway tubes, at first dismissed as unusable for shelter, were taken over by thousands of people who carried in bedding, reading materials, and food. Some lived there at night for weeks on end, coming out to go to work in the morning. Many Londoners found refuge in nearby towns, where churches and university halls were opened for public use. But workers had to stay close to the factories, and they suffered most from the bombing. Belatedly the government began work on shelters dug 80 to 105 feet underground, but these were not finished until the Blitz was over. Rescue, casualty, and fire services did tend to improve as the raids continued, but procuring water to fight fires was difficult, for it had to be drawn up from the Thames River.

Journalists' reports of British morale during the Blitz were often "dressed up," in part to win American support; sympathy for the British and antipathy for the Germans increased inordinately in the United States during this period. Not all the British were heroes and heroines during the raids, but basic discipline was maintained and rescue teams operated efficiently in seeking those trapped beneath bomb wreckage. Factory work resumed even after the severest of the raids. And the bombing did tend to break down the normal reticence of the English to mingle and talk with those of different class backgrounds. The bombings also promoted a sense of camaraderie among the thousands co-operating in the Home Guard, the rescue and stretcher parties, the casualty and fire services, the women's volunteer services, and those designated as air raid wardens.

OTHER BRITISH CITIES ATTACKED

German raids also affected other cities: Bristol, Birmingham, Southampton, Sheffield, Portsmouth, Leicester, Cardiff, Manchester, Belfast, and Plymouth suffered noticeable damage. A particularly infamous raid took place on Coventry on the night of November 14–15, 1940, killing 544 and seriously wounding 865. The assault destroyed a third of the city, which had twenty-one important factories, twelve of them directly concerned with aircraft manufacture. So deadly was the attack that the Germans coined the verb *coventrieren*—an action that produced virtual annihilation. Postwar research has destroyed the fable that Churchill knew of the plans for this raid and let it proceed without warning for fear the Germans would learn that the British project called Ultra had developed the capacity to break German secret military codes. The British had created devices that could replicate the operation of the complex Enigma machines used to code messages; at this stage of the war, however, the process of decoding was uncertain and time-consuming. The later breakthroughs in deciphering, much heralded in imaginative postwar literature, were very difficult to obtain.

London's worst hours came on December 29, 1940, and May 10, 1941, when incendiary bombs created extensive fires at a time when the Thames was low and fire-fighting services were virtually overwhelmed. Although London never suffered the firestorms that the British later inflicted on Hamburg and Dresden, streets were blocked by debris, and thousands of families were left without gas, water, and electricity. Serious loss of life resulted.

A kind of city pride in the ability to "take it" and survive developed during this period in spite of the German bombing. If

London could claim first place, it was followed closely by Coventry, Sheffield, Hull, Plymouth, Birmingham, Liverpool, and Bristol. After some raids morale was reported seriously shaken in Plymouth, Liverpool, and Portsmouth. With the commencement of the German invasion of the Soviet Union the incidence of German raids declined. But British efforts to retaliate came off badly in the early years—in 1941 the R.A.F. lost a bomber for every ten tons of bombs dropped, and more members of the R.A.F. died than did German civilians killed on the ground. This was also what the Germans termed a "happy time" for the submarines that were taking a heavy toll of British shipping, shortening the supplies of foodstuffs and raw materials so desperately needed.

THE FIRST AMERICAN MOVES
TOWARD ALLIANCE

British morale in this difficult period gained a boost with news of the beginning of American aid. In September 1940 President Roosevelt, still cautiously avoiding action which could be interpreted as a sign of an outright alliance with Britain, signed an agreement that provided the British with fifty American destroyers to assist in confronting the submarine menace. As a gesture of reciprocity, the British awarded six naval bases for the use of American forces. With Roosevelt's reelection in November 1940, isolationist sentiment began to weaken. The first direct step toward open aid to the British came in March 1941 with the passing of the Lend-Lease Act. This agreement made it possible for the United States to provide large quantities of foodstuffs (dried eggs, evaporated milk, bacon, canned meats, etc.) and fuel for the British at a time when Great Britain was enduring its most serious shortages of the war. Large quantities of war materiel also were shipped to Britain, and American naval forces helped to clear the seas of submarines haunting the supply lanes. In August 1941, at Placentia Bay, Newfoundland, Churchill had his first public meeting with Roosevelt. Here the two men agreed upon the phrasing of the Atlantic Charter, setting forth the goals which both men hoped would be realized at the end of the war.

During this same period the British gained an unexpected ally—the Soviet Union—when Hitler broke his non-aggression pact and invaded Russia on June 22, 1941. Churchill announced British support for the Russians, and the British public watched with admiration the resistance of the Russian people to the German invasion. Britain began to provide arms and materiel to the Soviet Union, and the United States extended Lend-Lease aid also. As a result of this circumstance, Communists in Great Britain were dealt with more tolerantly than they had been. Undoubtedly the greater acceptance of those on the left was accompanied by serious thought that victory in the war must result in greater social justice at home after the war.

Things continued to go badly on the high seas as the German cruisers *Scharnhorst* and *Gneisenau* were able to escape their winter harbors in France to raid commerce. More ominously, the British would have to confront still another enemy—the Japanese. Both the British and the Americans had watched the Japanese drive into China and then into French Indochina with concern but without the willingness to take outright military action. On July 24, 1941, the United States froze all Japanese assets in the United States, effectively shutting off that nation's importation of arms and oil. This action was followed by similar steps on the part of the British. The eventual consequence was the Japanese attack on the American naval forces in Pearl Harbor on December 7, 1941. Germany and Italy declared war on the United States a few days later, meaning that the British no longer stood alone. The formal partnership of these Anglo-Saxon nations, however, carried little immediate relief for the homeland. The British watched the rapid capture of their garrisons in Hongkong and Singapore with indications that military preparations in that area had been sadly lacking. And the sinking of the British battleships H.M.S. *Prince of Wales* and H.M.S. *Repulse* off the shores of Malaya constituted a real blow to British naval prestige.

THE DAYS OF AUSTERITY

Late in 1941 came the first military registration of women as well as men between the ages of eighteen and sixty. Some women between the ages of nineteen and thirty were called up for auxiliary services—mostly clerical or culinary—in the British armed forces.

For civilians at home wartime shortages grew worse by 1942. The Japanese victories cut off shipments of sugar, rice, and tea from the Far East. Now, three years into the war, austerity became the order of the day. Sir Stafford Cripps took over as Minister of Production in place of Lord Beaverbrook. No gasoline was now allowed for "pleasure motoring," but at the same time new bicycles to provide substitute transportation were virtually unavailable. Razor blades, condensed milk, breakfast cereal, soap, cosmetics, and clothing were all in short supply. With basic rations a man could buy a new pair of socks every four months, a pair of shoes every eight months, and a shirt every twenty months. Coal was in short supply. Bread production became standardized; the National Wheatmeal Loaf was described as "nasty, dirty, dark, coarse, and indigestible." Potatoes, however, were not rationed and were even served during tea time in scones. People also learned to eat some vegetables they had abhorred in prewar days. Chocolates and sweets were almost unobtainable. Some citizens still ate in restaurants on occasion. All restaurants, regardless of their prewar specialities, had to observe ration regulations. In addition, a number of state-run "British restaurants" offered basic fare at very reasonable prices. Many eating establishments could provide foods that could not be obtained in the markets, but rising prices made visits expensive for most people. There were, of course, stories of restaurants that still managed to cater to the wealthy, furnishing them with rich foods that had been enjoyed freely before the war. Everywhere in Europe (and also in the United States) some citizens were able to procure black market delicacies that others could only dream about. And those in country areas usually fared better than their city cousins.

The Germans still engaged in sporadic raids, choosing small towns so that the results were serious. Norwich, Bath, York, Exeter, and Canterbury were attacked. Even in 1943, the quietest year of the war for civilians, there was hardly a twenty-four hour period when there was not an air raid somewhere in Great Britain.

Factory work continued to carry long hours in plants still darkened for air raid protection. The women who were increasingly brought into factory labor were sometimes more dexterous in explosives and chemical factories than men. Other women worked in the Women's Land Army helping farmers keep up production. During this period farmers sought to clear and till areas which had been reserved for lawns and parks to add to their available acreage. City girls learned the joys of milking cows, felling trees, or helping to convert many acres of grass lands into plowed fields. But women still received smaller wages than men, and housewives who worked in factories often found insufficient restroom facilities, no provision for child care, and no allowance for them to take time to shop for the family. The war by no means destroyed traditional male-female relationships. In spite of the extended absence of men the birth rate rose, and it was difficult to obtain "prams" and baby baths.

On May 30, 1942, the British began the devastating air raids on German cities with the thousand-bomber raid on Cologne. It was the first of the area raids meant not only to knock out suspected munitions factories in German cities but also the residential areas of those who worked in them. Although the damage was not all that significant, the pattern was to be continued throughout the remainder of the war. From the first, there were some critical comments on the effectiveness of these raids. Nevertheless the R.A.F. Bomber Command refused to divert these planes to attacks on the submarine bases, which would probably have been ineffective, or to attacks on German oil supplies, which could not be pinpointed in the nighttime sorties to which the British bombers had to resort in view of the strength of German antiaircraft defenses.

Undoubtedly the British success in the second battle of El Alamein, on November 4, 1942, gained greater public notice and public satisfaction than did the bombing raids on German cities. It saved the Churchill regime from growing criticism, and General Sir Bernard Montgomery became the object of a perhaps overstated public hero worship. But British troops were no closer to invading the German homeland, and the disastrous raid on Dieppe on August 19, 1942, had indicated that an Allied move on to the Continent was still far off. Late in 1942 American forces joined the British to invade North Africa and secured the final victory against German forces in Africa. This was followed by the invasion of Sicily, the move up the Italian peninsula in 1943, and the departure of Italy from the Axis coalition. But the big news early in 1943 was of the surrender of German forces at Stalingrad, which betokened the coming of a major Russian counterattack. In Britain, there were celebrations for the Russian army, and the victory at Stalingrad led to the proclamation of a "Red Army Day."

AMERICAN TROOPS IN BRITAIN

Despite the good news from the battlefields, the year 1943 found the British at home increasingly weary and dispirited. As American troops began to arrive in Britain in 1943, they brought new problems for the British home front. Often the Americans were received with some hostility—they were "over-paid, over-sexed, and over here." By war's end 80,000 Englishwomen had become G.I. brides. Incidents of births out of wedlock and venereal disease also rose. The British were surprised at and critical of the racial discrimination displayed in the creation of segregated hostels and public houses. Although the Americans often drank up the short supply of beer and whiskey, they also provided coveted supplies of razor blades, cigarettes, and nylon stockings unavailable to their British hosts. The existing sense of overcrowding caused by the loss of housing and transfer of people from the cities into nearby towns was increased with the arrival of these foreign guests, even though construction of new military bases meant that few British citizens were displaced from homes or apartments.

Signs of nervousness, weariness, and short temper increased. The continuing blackouts, the difficulties of transport, the need to line up to get the necessities of life, the long hours of labor, and the dangerous work in the munitions factories all took their toll. Women continued to pour into the chemical factories, the explosives factories, the tank factories. Although not as many British women served in the armies as did their counterparts in Stalin's Russia, a larger percentage were enrolled in some kind of war work.

The government sought to cushion wartime hardships by providing a wider array of entertainment than had existed before the war. The radio provided some diversion for most Britishers. Even during air raids, the British Broadcasting Corporation (BBC), continued to air a regular slate of shows. Along with the news it provided music and comedy plays—notably ITMA, "It's That Man Again," starring Thomas Handley, who became the best-known radio personality of the war period. The imaginary figures of the show—Colonel Chinstrap, Mona Lot, and Mrs. Mopp—engaged in typical British repartee. Listeners could tune in a more intellectual performance and enjoy the "Three Wise Men," who answered audience questions and gave perspectives on science and philosophy. Few British listeners were able to tune their radios to the American Armed Forces Network, which provided swing music and comedy that probably would not have been popular among the majority of the British listeners. The BBC also provided chamber music for the entertainment of workers during their lunch period in the factory.

It was the movies that gained the most popularity during the war period. British actors enjoyed more popularity than those of Hollywood. J. Arthur Rank became the best-known producer of this period. Workers attended at noon or whenever they could find free time. Cinema organists would often play popular favorites like "White Cliffs of Dover" and "Lili Marlene" before the show. "Lili Marlene" was a haunting, lovesick ballad that British soldiers had picked up from German radio broadcasts for troops in North Africa. It had a considerable popularity in America as well as in Great Britain. Other entertainments such as soccer and cricket retained their appeal during the war. Crowds attended in spite of the danger of bombing raids.

Education suffered greatly during the war. Teachers and students were drafted, and the normal school schedule disrupted. A shortage of paper and printing facilities limited research and publication in non-scientific fields. Some effort was made to improve the education of army recruits, but the results were not satisfactory. Criticisms of the prewar elitist educational system persisted, but reform was not forthcoming until after 1945.

On the other hand, British scientists contributed such vital technology as radar and improved, more accurate bomb sights. They also helped improve the defensive capabilities of both British and American bombers. Paints for camouflage, synthetic rubber production, and atomic research were but a few of the contributions. Nevertheless, British military leaders never fully accepted the counsel of civilian scientists.

PREPARATIONS FOR THE INVASION OF THE CONTINENT

By June 1944 one-and-a-half million American servicemen occupied prefabricated huts, tents, and some buildings in Britain. To this human cargo was added five million tons of supplies and armaments stored around the perimeter of the island. Roads and beaches were covered with planes, tanks, trucks, ammunition, and food supplies. The sight of all this material abundance produced envy in some British citizens, a condition reduced somewhat by the generosity of American soldiers who offered money, candy, chewing gum, and cigarettes. British war production had begun to decline somewhat in the latter stages of the war, increasing strain upon the working population and forcing greater dependence upon American imports. To boost morale and raise productivity, Churchill had even recommended some reduction of the blackout regulations to decrease the number of accidents befalling workers because of the dim nighttime conditions. But the Germans dashed these attempts by carrying out a new "little Blitz" in the early months of 1944, using incendiaries to attack London, Hull, Bristol, and South Wales.

Meanwhile, British intelligence had learned of German preparations to produce flying bombs and long-distance rockets. The latter created the most concern. On the night of August 17, 1943, 571 British bombers carried out a largely successful attack on the German installations at Peenemunde on the coast of the Baltic Sea. Although the raid did not completely destroy the operations, it did force the Germans to move to underground works in the Hartz Mountains. Experimental use of the weapons was reported early in 1944, and details of the weapons were learned from a rocket captured by Polish intelligence sources in July of that year.

But it was the flying bomb, the German V-1 (the "V" stood for *Vergeltung*, vengeance) that provided widespread concern to the British public. Knowledge of this weapon had also come to

British intelligence sources before 1944. Attacks on suspected launching sites on the French coast had been carried out before the invasion of the Continent was launched on June 6, 1944. But the Germans were able to create new launching sites for the V-1. Exactly one week after D-Day, the first of the V-1's fell on greater London. The inhabitants of that city soon came to know they were in danger when they heard the telltale sound of this "buzz bomb." It was a jet-propelled projectile that reached speeds of up to four hundred miles per hour. When it exploded above the ground, its ton of high explosives was capable of wreaking heavy damage over a large area. The first line of defense against these weapons involved the effort of fighter planes to knock out these small and speedy objects before they entered the range of anti-aircraft fire and increased the risk of serious damage. To provide earlier interception, antiaircraft batteries with 1,000 guns were moved to the coast, and additional barrage balloons were raised. Some 6,700 V-1's were launched against London; 3,500 were destroyed before landing, but 2,400 of them struck civilian areas, killing 6,184 people and injuring seriously 12,981.

The buzz bombs provided a new pressure on a population already battered by conventional bombing. V-1's could strike at any time of day or night. In spite of the buzzing sound, one had little time to go to shelters. When one heard the "buzz," one "hit the dirt." But bombing of the launching sites gradually reduced frequency of attacks, and as British forces moved on into France, they overran the launching sites. Even then the Germans were still able to release 750 more of the pesky weapons from airplanes.

The more serious weapon, the V-2, was the first genuine guided missile used during the war. The "flying gas-mains," as the British called them, were twelve feet long and carried a ton of explosives in their warheads. Conventional aircraft were powerless to stop them, and they arrived at their target soundlessly. Development of this truly "vengeance-minded" weapon had been delayed by the attack on Peenemunde in 1943 and came only after Allied bombing and opening of the western front had rendered launching sites in northern France unusable. Consequently V-2's launched against Great Britain had to be launched from Belgium and were not as accurate as they might have been had they been launched from the prepared sites in France. As it was, 1,300 were directed towards England and 500 hit London, resulting in 2,724 deaths and 6,467 serious injuries.

The destruction created by both types of bombs added more housing problems to those occasioned by conventional bombing. Little wonder that most British citizens felt little remorse for the damage to German cities caused by British saturation bombing. The accuracy and speed of the V-2's made them more deadly than the buzz bombs had been, and only Germany's collapse prevented the V-2's from being more catastrophic. The missiles provided a harsh ending to the long siege of London from the air.

The signs of impending triumph were accompanied by signs of domestic unrest. British citizens could take pride in the valiant role played by their troops in the bitter, hard-fought campaigns in Italy and Normandy. Popular acclaim for General Montgomery continued to grow, although the Americans were not convinced that he possessed superior military talents. But the victory that ended World War II was to a considerable degree an American one. Britain had had to draw heavily upon the goodwill of the United States for arms, foodstuffs, ammunition, and its much greater resources of manpower. To a very considerable degree Britain emerged from the war bankrupt, its resources expended by six years of total war. It staked a legitimate claim for continued aid in the postwar period. The war had also broken the privilege of social position and outmoded class distinctions. The effective prosecution of the war had required involvement and sacrifice by all classes. In its postwar reconstruction plans, the British determined to eradicate feudal systems of military and social leadership in Germany, Italy, and Japan. At home there was also to be a commitment to greater social justice. Early in 1943 the Liberal social planner, Sir William Beveridge, had presented a plan for universal social security to be paid for by those enrolled in it. At the time it received marginal support from the government, but these ideas became the foundation of Britain's welfare state. For the first time the people of England had a truly popular newspaper, *The Daily Mirror*, which reflected the thoughts and the hopes of the masses; it was enjoyed by the working classes in particular. Most of its readership hoped for better living conditions after the war, but they rarely articulated specific objectives. One exception was the miners, who had been engaged in the hardest and most dangerous work during the war, laboring in obsolescent and often unsafe conditions. Their restlessness in the last years of the war led them to advocate government ownership of the mines as a way of ridding themselves of harsh private management. Educational reform allowing a larger degree of free, public education had been adopted in 1944–45. Winston Churchill had symbolized the pride of the British in their days of challenge, but before the final victory over the Japanese he lost his majority in the House of Commons to Clement Attlee, who stood for a new era in which the rewards of victory were to come to the working man as well as the traditional governing class. But with the challenge of wartime survival past, the creation of a postwar symbiosis of Labour and Conservative forces proved much more difficult. The onset of the Cold War required a renewed commitment on Britain's part to maintain military strength and political influence in western Europe, lest the Continent fall completely under the influence of the Soviet Union. The aftermath of victory for the British was characterized by many years of political swings between excessive nationalization of business and doggedly conservative regimes.

2 / THE SOVIET UNION

Nowhere in World War II was the fighting more cruel, more devastating than it was in the Soviet Union. Germany and the Soviet Union lost literally millions of soldiers. The savagery of the conflict shattered all assumed standards of modern warfare; both sides executed thousands of prisoners of war and forced hundreds of thousands of others to march to harsh prison camps ill-provided with food and shelter. The distinction between soldiers and civilians tended to disappear. Millions of Russian civilians were forcibly "recruited" for work in German armament industries. Additional millions of Russian civilians who became soldiers when their home area was attacked had been workers in the armament factories until that time. Survival on both sides was often purchased at the cost of pitiless savagery.

Before the war the Soviet Union had shared in the eyes of western governments a dark and forbidding reputation that rivaled that of Nazi Germany. Through the 1920s and 1930s the stories of the harshness and cruelty of the regime enjoyed wide currency. The accounts of the misdeeds of the GPU ("Gay-Pay-OO," as the pronounciation was rendered in the newspapers) and its successor the NKVD resembled those detailing the savagery of the Gestapo and the SS. The dictatorship on the left seemed little different from the dictatorship on the right except that the former worked to destroy capitalism, while the latter seemed to preserve it, but only to serve the goals of its aggressive foreign policy. Observers tended to believe that Hitler's hatred of communism would prevent him from joining hands with Stalin's regime. In 1939 it was clear that the leading diplomats of France and Great Britain had discounted this possibility.

There was, however, one overriding similarity between the two regimes. Both were controlled by dictators who had achieved complete personal control over their party agencies and the governmental apparatus which they directed. Joseph Stalin had succeeded Nikolai Lenin (V. I. Ulyanov) as head of the Soviet Communist Party. Although he praised Lenin's accomplishments, he created a state that was probably far different from that which Lenin had contemplated. During the late 1920s and the 1930s Stalin sought to eradicate the existence of independent peasants and replace their holdings with collective and state farms; those who opposed this move became the first prisoners in a great complex of forced labor camps. Optimistic and often poorly conceived Five Year Plans spurred the production of iron and steel but left many items of ordinary use in short supply. And over both the people and the party itself Stalin placed a secret police system that operated harshly and unpredictably, sometimes turning upon well-known party leaders, and even pouncing on those who had carried out the liquidations. In the two years before World War II Stalin purged many of the party and military leaders to eliminate any potential opposition. Moreover, as Nikita Khrushchev indicated after the war, Stalin had created a cult of personality that was to be immensely strengthened during the war.

As a consequence, the events of August, 1939, which saw the ruthless dictators of the two ideologically opposed states joining in a pact of friendship, provided a massive shock to western observers but stirred little internal concern or opposition in either Germany or Russia. For most of the first two years of World War II, the Soviet Union was virtually an ally of Nazi Germany. In the secret protocol of the Non-Aggression Pact of August 24, 1939, the two partners had agreed upon the division of Poland. The Soviet Union received control of over one-third of the country; at the end of the war the Soviet diplomats would claim that this area had been Russian territory before 1914 and was unjustly awarded to the new Polish state. But at the same time that Soviet forces occupied their portion of Poland, they also moved to recover control of the Baltic states of Estonia, Latvia, and Lithuania. In November 1939 the Soviet Union became involved in an unexpectedly difficult war to force Finland to grant territory along the border north of Leningrad, as well as protective territory far to the north along the frontier with Norway. The Soviets also demanded control of the Hangoe Islands protecting the entry into the Gulf of Finland. These results were achieved by March 1940, at considerable loss of life and equipment. Throughout this period of collaboration the Soviet Union continued to provide Germany with millions of tons of grain, timber, and petroleum products along with significant quantities of cotton, manganese, and chromium.

During these two years of informal alliance the Soviets did have some concern over German designs in the Balkans. Fearing future aggression, some efforts were made to fortify the defenses in the new areas gained by the Nazi-Soviet pact. But the damages to the military leadership from the purge period of 1937–1939, which may have taken the lives of 15,000 officers, had not been repaired. Consequently Stalin was deprived of military intelligence and advice that might have prepared him better for the German invasion. The new territories gained in the west had not been well integrated into the Soviet defenses. Meanwhile, thousands of citizens of eastern Poland and many of the Balts were joining various other prisoners in the Gulag Archipelago, the great complex of prison camps in the eastern Soviet Union that held a million-and-a-half prisoners in early 1941.

Recent research has indicated that the Soviet Union was, prior to the German invasion, actively preparing for war. By June 1941, there were 5.4 million Soviet citizens in uniform, and Soviet industry was producing each month 230 tanks, 700 military aircraft, 4,000 guns and mortars, and more than 100,000 rifles, a total considerably greater than the output of Nazi Germany. But much of this production was located in the Soviet Union's vulnerable territories in the south and west. Stalin had rebuffed British and American warnings of Hitler's intention to strike. Although postwar scholarship indicates that Stalin expected war with Germany by 1942, it is also clear that the massive German invasion on June 22, 1941, was unexpected and that no significant strategic contingencies had been prepared to counter it. The Soviet military leaders had seen the results of the air power in the west but had not moved to provide antiaircraft defense for their cities or taken action to enhance the capacity of existing airfields. Most significantly, the Soviet military had failed to take steps to move their most vital military industries to more secure areas and neglected to expand and upgrade the railroad system. One can only reflect that provision of more serious warnings to troops on the front line might have mitigated the atmosphere of utter surprise that accompanied the German invasion of June 22, 1941.

RAPIDITY OF GERMAN CONQUESTS

Even in retrospect, the massive invasion that Hitler launched against the Soviet Union overwhelms the imagination. One hundred forty-eight German divisions, nineteen of them armored, twelve motorized, pierced a border area stretching 1,800 miles north and south. This force included 3,350 tanks, 7,184 artillery pieces, 60,000 heavy trucks, and 700,000 horses to move light artillery pieces and baggage trains. Calling this invasion a great European campaign against Communism, Hitler had enlisted aid from Italy, Rumania, Hungary, Finland, and Slovakia with some contingents from the Dutch, Flemish, Valonians, Norwegians, and Ukrainians. Help also came from the Baltic states, France, and Spain later. These forces thrust eastward in three groups, north, center, and south. The northern group was expected to take Leningrad and cut railroads to Moscow, the center group to take Minsk and Smolensk and eventually occupy Moscow, and the southern group to seize agricultural areas and eventually to expropriate the oil resources of the Caucasus mountain region. The German forces were led by well-known and experienced commanders, Ritter von Leeb, Fedor von Bock, and Gerd von Rundstedt. They were faced by 170 Russian divisions supported by 6,000 planes and 54 armored brigades, each having 200 tanks. These tanks, however, were mostly obsolete models. Worse still, the 1,475 newly developed T-34s, which proved later so efficient, were at the time operated by inexperienced drivers. Much of the Soviet air force was destroyed on the ground in the early days of the invasion. Thousands of tanks and perhaps a million soldiers were lost. In the first few weeks German armies moved all the way to the vicinity of Leningrad, Kiev, and Smolensk. In eighteen days Hitler's forces had moved 400 miles into the Soviet interior and were less than 200 miles from Moscow. Not until the latter part of 1943 did Soviet forces cease fighting a defensive war with enormous losses of men and materiel.

Very early in the campaign German soldiers began to suffer heavy losses of men and morale. It is true that many of them felt a sense of mission in clearing this primitive and backward area of "inferior" Slavs so that Germans could be resettled there. Yet the opposition they confronted from the Soviet military and guerrilla bands robbed units of their most experienced officers and non-coms, thus destroying the esprit de corps. By September the German troops were facing the onset of winter. Mists, rain, and heavy snow converted the roads into mushy tracks so that tanks and trucks stalled, while soldiers dressed in summertime uniforms suffered from the cold.

Besides the strictly military operation, the Germans embarked on an extensive racial war. *Sicherheitsdienst* ("Security Service," a branch of the SS) units followed the army to secure the territory won, to eliminate Jewish and Communist party elements, and to prepare the way for a "proper" Nazi administration of the conquered territory. Although these party units were supposed to operate discreetly, in practice the army frequently witnessed the slaughter and executions. This spectacle of savagery, coupled with the hardships of the fighting, the loss of pride in their units, and the fear of enemy reprisals, brutalized military units in a way not seen in the war in western Europe.

From the very first, the war became for the citizens of the Soviet Union a national war, a total war in which the line of separation between soldiers and civilians virtually disappeared. Although some nationalities had hoped that German conquest might mean liberation from the cruel hardships of the Communist regime, these hopes were quickly disappointed. German military administrators and apparently many troops regarded Slavs as backward, inferior people to be exploited by the *Herrenvolk*. As German forces occupied Soviet territory, Russian Jews were gathered up and destroyed. Thousands of Russians, Ukrainians, Byelorussians, and others were shipped back to Germany to perform enforced labor. Soviet soldiers captured by the Germans were sent on foot to prisoner of war camps, where they received little food and almost no medical aid. Thousands of them were to die in these camps. Their plight frequently became known to the Russian civilians in the area and helped to stir up and add strength to the partisan forces confronting the Germans. The invaders responded by burning small towns along their path, executing summarily any suspected of resistance, and confiscating food supplies.

STALIN'S "PATRIOTIC WAR"

The first public notice to the Soviet people of the German invasion came in the radio address of Foreign Minister Vyacheslav Molotov, not from Stalin. Stalin was in deep despair during the first days of the invasion. By July 3, however, he rallied and addressed the nation by radio. From the first he sought to describe the war as a national war, a war of the people—"our patriotic war of liberation against the Fascist enslavers." And, somehow, for many Russians Stalin became the symbol of popular feelings. Before the war he had been a relatively shadowy figure. In the official war reports he became the personification of the Soviet spirit of patriotism and of military valor in the defense of Moscow, Leningrad, and Stalingrad. He was to receive the same kind of poetic deification that had been accorded to Hitler. In many respects his war leadership resembled that of the Führer. Stalin spent the war in the security of a bombshelter 115 feet below the surface, protected by steel doors and booby traps. Like Hitler, he did not visit the battlefield often—historians know of only one such visit. But like Hitler also, he used the telephone to keep in close touch with his field commanders and determined much of the battle strategy. Before the end of the war he selected capable commanders to replace those whose incompetence in the earlier stages of the war was beyond question.

Soviet propaganda increasingly emphasized the collective spirit of the Russian people. Like the British, the Russians truly confronted the dangers of warfare as a unified people (although Ukrainians and the Asiatic peoples of the east were never securely tied to the Russian cause). But unlike the British, the Russian people were subject to a totalitarian government that had placed millions of its subjects in concentration camps. The people worked, suffered, and survived because they had no real choice to do otherwise. Aleksandr Solzhenitsyn detailed in *The Gulag Archipelago* the punishment of those soldiers who surrendered to the German armies. Civilians who remained in German controlled areas were likely to be arrested by the Russians when those territories were recaptured. Yet there was indeed evidence that an élan, a spirit of courageous solidarity, like that which animated the British, was evident in the Soviet Union. It derived from a deep-seated love of the native soil that withstood all of the harshness of the Soviet system. Moreover the state did make some significant concessions to popular feelings; most notably the government moderated its anti-religion stance and permitted some return to the solace of the Russian Orthodox Church.

Journalists gave considerable praise to partisans who harried the German forces as they moved deep into unfamiliar plains and forests. These deeds of heroism were noted in the pages of the official reports, most notably those frontline dispatches from Ilya Ehrenburg. It remains puzzling that Ehrenburg's descriptions have been supplemented by so relatively few personal accounts. Memoirs of wartime civilians are virtually nonexistent, in sharp contrast to Great Britain. As a consequence, the great struggle, which required the sacrifices and sufferings of millions of Soviet citizens, remains a shadowy panorama to historians. Recent research in the wake of Communism's collapse has firmed up some details of those trials and sufferings.

THE YEARS OF DEFEAT: 1941–1942

The first two years of the war were for the people of the Soviet Union a time when the basic survival of the state was seriously imperilled. During this period, one-third of the Soviet population was under German control. Agriculture and food supplies fell by three-fifths as the Germans occupied the best agricultural lands of the state. Supplies of household necessities and clothing dwindled to less than two-thirds of previous levels. Rationing was instituted, but the system established favored the military and those working in vital industries. White-collar workers, except for those working for the party, tended to receive minimal rations, and dependents and children were left with very little. Even then the basic bread ration, which had been the most significant staple of the Russian diet, often could not be met. Potatoes often were substituted for it, especially for the peasants. Some living in rural areas managed to obtain extras from "local resources." Frequently they were peasants who raised vegetables, pigs, and poultry, or workers on the collective farms, who produced surplus food from private plots. The intrusion of German forces quickly reduced these supplies, however. Wherever the German forces arrived, they confiscated all the food stocks of the collectives and provided some very minimal rations for those who worked on them. Often they drove out women and children into the cold of winter without any food.

The Soviet state took strong action to combat natural disaster and the invaders. Hunger and disease, particularly typhus, typhoid fever, and tuberculosis were rampant. Against these diseases the state was to provide 250 million innoculations in the first two years of the fighting. The dangers of defeatism were countered as well. Police and army units shot thousands for spreading rumors of the strength of the German forces. Soviet civilians who surrendered to the Germans were threatened with death, and sometimes these reprisals were carried out. Efforts were made to recruit a people's militia—on paper there were more than four million volunteers. The peasants, who had been the least attached to Stalin's system, had their solidarity weakened by mass enrollment in the military forces—they were to constitute 60 percent of the Soviet armed forces. Many others were drafted into industrial work.

Because the Ukrainians had shown a considerable predilection to accept German rule, the Soviet government acted to crush other nationalist aspirations. Nearly 400,000 ethnic Germans of the Volga region were deported to Siberia and Central Asia; Crimean Tatars and Moslem and Turkish nationalities in the Caucasus regions were also subjected to relocation, a trend that continued throughout the war. Those who had aided the Nazis, the so-called *Hilfswillige*, "little helpers," were often shot when they fell into the hands of the Soviets.

The territories that Germans occupied in these early years had also housed a very sizeable portion of the Soviet industrial complex. More than 85 percent of the U.S.S.R.'s prewar aircraft factories, 70 percent of its coking coal and iron ore resources, and 60 percent of its pig iron, coal, and aluminum industrial complex were swallowed up by the Germans before the tide of battle began to change. Shortly after the German invasion, the

Soviet leadership began to move millions of workers and relocated factories to secure areas beyond the Urals. This massive movement of people created a whole new complex of industrial cities in western Asia, but the effort required to accomplish this enormous movement of people and materiel was tremendous; it was partially depicted in one of the propaganda movies of the period. Some factories were back in operation less than two weeks after the beginning of the move despite the difficulties in rebuilding them on the cold and frozen soil. Eight thousand railroad cars were required to evacuate one of the steel mills, the materials carried weighing 50,000 tons. In all some 1,360 large war plants were moved to the east by October 1941, a total of 1,523 by the end of the year. News reports of the time lionized these participants in this great movement of men and materiel as emulators of the prewar ideal of Soviet accomplishments—they were new Stakhanovites (the term used in the 1930s for miners and factory workers who greatly exceeded their required quotas) achieving more than was humanly possible under normal circumstances. Recent research has indicated that the wartime portrayals of this great Soviet feat were overblown—serious shortages of transport, road links, electric power lines, sources of metals and component parts for some industries hampered the operation of the transferred factories. Inadequate rail transportation also handicapped military actions. Housing and food supplies for the workers in these new industrial complexes remained meager for most of the war.

Perhaps the strongest rallying point for Russian resistance in this period of trial was personal hatred for the Germans. The intruders were likened to vermin and bacilli. A wartime poem suggested there was only one way to deal with a German: "Kill Him!" There was also a strong sense of personal and national pride that kept survivors going in the midst of the most cruel circumstances. A sentimental song of the period voiced a mystical belief that faith in the survival of loved ones would bring them safely back at the end of the conflict.

Stalin's appeal to patriotism was most notably underscored in the most dramatic scenes of the conflict—those surrounding the survival of the city of Leningrad, the defense of Moscow, and the German defeat in the Crimea.

The city of Leningrad became "the hero city" of the Soviet Union by virtue of the tenacious resistance of its people under the most extreme hardships faced anywhere during World War II. The German armies had pushed through the former Baltic states to cut off the entire southern boundary of this city of nearly three million people. The northern boundary of the city fronted on territory reclaimed by Finnish troops, who did not participate in the later bombardments of the city but who also did not allow the Soviets to acquire food or supplies from that direction. The only supply line for Leningrad lay across the waters of Lake Ladoga to the east, but when German forces seized territory south of the lake, supplies had to come from areas to the north or east having only primitive railroad connections or truck routes. More danger came from the constant surveillance and attack of German airplanes over Lake Ladoga itself.

The failure to evacuate the civilian population and armament factories of Leningrad was one of the many Soviet mistakes in the early days of the German invasion. The unpreparedness of the city indicates that military leaders had clearly miscalculated the strength and swiftness of the German advance. Hundreds of thousands of the Leningraders, including old women and young girls, were sent out to build fortifications. The size and scope of these defensive lines—340 miles of antitank ditches and 5,875 miles of open trenches—reflect the enormous labor involved. But these preparations were inadequate for combating the effects of a long-term siege. Food especially was in short supply as the noose tightened. As a consequence the millions of Leningraders faced the winter in 1941 under constant bombardment from a persistent foe, enduring severe cold and declining supplies of coal and electricity, and most seriously of all, watching food supplies shrink to miniscule quantities through those bleak, frigid days. Some supplies had been brought in across Lake Ladoga in the autumn months, but German forces cut off the railroad supply lines to the south, forcing the Russians to rely on infrequent air drops to keep the city from starvation.

By November 1941 food supplies in Leningrad sank to critical levels. Rations provided a scanty 1,000 calories a day for workers; others received little better than half that amount. Deaths from hunger and cold skyrocketed. Some estimates place the total number of deaths during the siege at 900,000. Coffins were almost unavailable. Hundreds of corpses were taken to cemeteries and abandoned. Some Leningraders tried to escape across Lake Ladoga when it was frozen, but in their weakened condition few made it to safety. The soldiers defending the city fared somewhat better than the civilians, although their rations, too, were meager.

The freezing of Lake Ladoga and the later recapture by the Russians of the key railroad junction of Tikhvin to the south alleviated the worst of the shortages, although hardships continued well into 1942. Cold continued to cause many deaths. Wooden furniture and wooden houses were burned for fuel. Water pipes froze, and people died from exposure while waiting in outdoor lines for rations. The constant bombing of factories and homes added to the mortality rates. The Kirov works, which had made optical lenses, retooled to produce hand grenades, antitank mines, small arms, and machine guns throughout the blockade; it became a prime target for German artillery and bombers. Workers stumbled through the streets to their work benches and sometimes died on the road or even at their work places. Fewer male workers were available, but their places had to be filled with more women and girls. Ultimately the plant survived.

Alexander Werth has described the doggedness of the city's inhabitants in their efforts to survive. As he points out, there was no real alternative for the citizens of Leningrad—surrender would have subjected the city to a barbaric Nazi occupation, for Leningrad was the symbol of the Soviet Union and international Communism. But fear was not the only motivator. Leningraders had a deep attachment to their city and prided themselves on their maintenance of discipline in the face of impossible odds.

Leningrad's stoic heroism contrasted sharply with the near-panic occasioned in Moscow as the Germans approached the city. On October 16, 1941, thousands of Muscovites fled to surrounding areas without authorization. Within days, however, despite the proximity of German forces, morale was restored, partially due to Stalin's famous speech in which he appealed to the history of "the great Russian nation." Stalin linked the name of Lenin with the famous artists and scholars of Russia: Pushkin, Tolstoy, Chekhov, Tchaikovsky, and Pavlov, along with

Russian generals Suvorov and Kutuzov. By the end of November, Moscow was again secure, and German forces had lost some three-quarters of a million men in their campaigns around the city. The inhabitants of the smaller cities around Moscow often suffered fearfully—the Germans executed those considered to be dangerous, consumed all their food supplies, and burned down their houses when they evacuated them.

During 1942 Hitler shifted his campaign to the south. Sebastopol became a center of resistance in the same way Leningrad had. After the German invasion had cleared out much of the surrounding area, the siege of this major city on the Black Sea began on October 30, 1941. Defended on land by strong fortifications and on the water by portions of the Soviet navy, the city held out against strong German pressure. Most of the civilian population was moved into underground cellars and caves while the Germans bombed the city above them. Munitions were made and schools conducted beneath the besieged city. By the end of 1941, the Germans had lost some battles around Sebastopol, and inhabitants of the city assumed their enemy was defeated. People emerged from the caves and began to rebuild houses and restore lines of transportation.

Then on May 20, 1942, the Germans took the area around Kerch and began a new offensive against Sebastopol. Some evacuations began, but many residents of the city remained, again living underground through renewed and more devastating bombardment. Added to air attack was the thunder of a giant siege gun called "Dora." During the final days of the siege, the stench of unburied bodies was so overpowering that Sebastopol's defenders had to wear gas masks. In July the Germans at last occupied the wrecked city.

THE ROLE OF ALLIED AID

During these days of trauma, Great Britain had moved quickly to form an alliance with the Soviet Union, while the United States, not yet a warring power, made the Soviet Union eligible to receive Lend-Lease aid. Throughout the war and afterwards apologists for the Soviet Union charged that the western democracies had not provided sufficient assistance to the U.S.S.R. in the midst of its most serious difficulties. In fact the United States and Great Britain sent to the Soviet Union in the period from October 1, 1941, to May 31, 1945, 2,660 ships carrying 15,234,791 long tons of cargo, including 427,284 trucks, 13,303 combat vehicles, 35,170 motorcycles, 2,328 ordnance service vehicles, 2,670,371 tons of petroleum products, 4,478,116 tons of foodstuffs, 1,900 steam locomotives, 66 diesel locomotives, 9,920 flat cars, 1,000 dump cars, and a billion dollars worth of machinery and industrial equipment. Hundreds of aircraft were also supplied, many of them at a time when the United States itself was in early stages of its own rearmament. All of these supplies had to be delivered over dangerous paths to the Soviet Union. Undoubtedly these supplies were vital to the survival of the Soviet state.

More troublesome than the quantities of Lend-Lease aid was the Soviet pressure on the United States and Great Britain to open a second front. Stalin moreover insisted that the only condition acceptable to the Soviet Union was a direct frontal assault on the German-occupied coastline of France. Only such an invasion, the Soviets declared, could alleviate the continuing pressure of German forces on Soviet territory. Such logic, however, assumed that the democratic states were willing to impose upon their citizens the profligate loss of life that had been suffered by Soviet forces. Moreover, American leaders were divided on whether the war in Europe was the primary objective of American policy, since the Japanese had directly provoked the U.S. entry into the war. Because the prospective road to victory in the Far East loomed as a long and rocky journey, it was argued that the European war should be finished first.

FALL 1942: THE TIDE BEGINS TO TURN

The year 1942 began with new German victories. Hitler's troops penetrated deeply into the Caucasus region. As noted above, Sebastopol fell into the hands of the Germans by July, along with much of the Crimean peninsula. The Germans seemed on the verge of taking over the vital oilfields in that area. But by this time Soviet military production was beginning to recover. Thousands of women had now entered the work force. By 1942 they constituted 52 percent of all factory workers. They were joined by considerable numbers of former peasants and by many young people only fourteen or fifteen years old. The inexperience of these new industrial recruits meant, of course, that production climbed rather slowly. Likewise, replacements for miners who had been drafted were often unfit for the demanding tasks they faced. The party oversaw this mobilization of the civilian population for war work, but in the light of the desperate situation of the country those determinations were accepted more willingly than in prewar days. Occasionally coercion was exercised, but all accounts seem to support a view that the populace accepted the sacrifices needed to free the homeland. The party made strong efforts to stir productivity and return to the Stakhanovite standards of prewar days. Propaganda pushed workers to reach 200 percent of the established norms, then 300 percent, and finally 1000 percent. Komsomol (Communist youth) brigades sought to instill military discipline in the factories, complete with military oaths, a hierarchy of command, and managerial decisions by vote.

During this period even the numbers in the prison camps declined. Some died from the hardships and casualities of areas in battle zones. Still, there were fewer arrests, and a considerable sum of prisoners were released to service in penal battalions, where they could fight the enemy rather than suffer a likely death in prison. And after 1942 the partisan movement obtained military equipment and training from the Soviet authorities. Although the partisans were in some respects forced to do the Soviets' bidding, most willingly fulfilled their "quotas" such as killing at least five "fascists," taking part in three guerilla actions per month, and rescuing their wounded comrades from possible capture by the enemy. They began to attack frequently enemy supply lines by derailing German trains and shooting the soldiers using them.

The Germans responded by providing armor and increased protection for many trains. More important, they also sought new allies among the Cossacks, Turkmenians, Uzbeks, Azerbaizans, Armenians, Georgians, and other disaffected nationalities. One of the great failures of Hitler's invasion of Russia was the Nazis' unwillingness to exploit popular discontent with Stalinism and allow these elements to assist the German armies.

Clearly the Germans might well have found allies and support in the Soviet Union had not their racial world view and contempt for all non-German peoples stood in the way of some kind of reasonable partnership.

Meanwhile, there continued to be errors and shortcomings in the Communist party's management of wartime needs. These were scarcely surprising in view of the overwhelming problems that had to be confronted. Some fifty-five evacuated factories that had not been taken by the Germans were still idle at the end of 1942. Some experienced factory workers had been conscripted at the outset of the invasion, but by the end of 1941 they were returning increasingly to the factories to contribute their skills to the war effort. The conscription of railroad workers was finally halted in May 1942 and some laborers were released from the military to keep the supply trains in motion.

Soviet production of arms rose dramatically after 1941. Production figures doubled in 1942, and by 1944 the figures stood four times higher than those of 1940. But output was uneven. In 1942 the artillary endured a famine of shells, a condition largely remedied by the next year. But the most significant boost came in 1942 with the return of experienced Soviet military forces from the Far East, which until that time had been pinned down awaiting a Japanese move into Manchuria. These tough soldiers stiffened the Soviet resolve.

It was, of course, the defense of Stalingrad in late 1942 and early 1943 that turned the tide of battle. The story of the heroic defense of that city rivals that of Leningrad as one of the high points of Soviet history. But Stalingrad was the saga of the Soviet armies, not civilians. It was, of course, the beginning of the rollback of German armies from Soviet territory. After February 1943, the Red Army was no longer on the defensive, and the liberation of Russian soil was virtually completed before the invasion of France by the western Allies.

Not until June 6, 1944, did the Soviets get their long hoped-for second front. But even before that time some German forces had been pulled out of Russia to meet the Allied campaign in Italy. Before the end of 1944, Russian forces had moved into Rumania and Poland and later into Hungary and Czechoslovakia. By this time also Soviet aims for security had been clearly defined as the communization of all the states along the U.S.S.R.'s frontiers. As Soviet armies reconquered lost territory they expelled or imprisoned those whom they regarded as hostile to their cause and returned full measure of the brutality that they had suffered from their invaders. As they moved into Poland and then into Germany itself, thousands of refugee Germans fled fearing the cruelty and rape that some Red Army units were perpetrating. Indeed, the harshness of Soviet occupation in the immediate postwar period hastened the onset of the Cold War. Western admiration for Soviet heroism reverted to prewar fears of Stalinist totalitarianism and the Communist take over of all Europe.

Every postwar newsreel of the Soviet Union has been replete with views of war monuments celebrating the victories of Soviet forces and the heroism of its soldiers. The sincerity of this admiration for Soviet heroism cannot be doubted. Nine million Soviet soldiers died in the war. Some nineteen million civilians also perished. Many, perhaps most of them, died for the "motherland" and for Stalin, who represented the state, the homeland, the nation, as well as the Communist party. World War II left behind a lasting pride in survival and victory, a feat attributed to Stalin and his military leaders. Left behind also was an excessive respect for the military and dominant role for the Russian nationality in the Soviet Union. Serious losses of industrial capacity and of infrastructure were not completely restored. The family was weakened, and birth rates declined. The Soviet intelligentsia suffered losses that it never recovered. Those areas that had been overrun by the Germans and recovered were never fully integrated into the postwar state. Much of the work force remained inexperienced and improperly trained well into the postwar period. The Cold War mentality delayed economic recovery, and the Communist party, which had developed some flexibility during the fighting, reverted to its earlier rigidity.

The history of World War II has been presented in a number of official Soviet presentations since the end of the conflict. Until recently the contributions of its ordinary citizens were not fully described, and the full range of the enormous suffering as well as accurate counts of lives lost were not yet fully disclosed. Official histories and statistics need to be fleshed out by the personal narratives that could not be published under a totalitarian regime. Perhaps with the recent monumental changes in the Soviet Union, missing details of this story may now be revealed at last.

3 / FRANCE: UNDER THE GERMAN HEEL

France was only one of many states defeated and occupied by the Germans in World War II, but it was the only Great Power to lie under the heel of the Nazi boot. Its defeat overcame the country with a sense of failure and disgrace, and its citizens seriously questioned the validity of republican government. France had entered the twentieth century with multiple traditions. The aura of the former monarchy and of the two Napoleonic regimes, along with the memories of military greatness, were joined by the emergence of socialism and the rise of a new left-wing cultural tradition that was popular among intellectuals. As a consequence the Third French Republic witnessed in its seventy-year history (1870–1940) a complex pattern of contrasting trends, forces, and accomplishments.

France was a victor in World War I. But its good fortune was not the product of great military leadership. Ultimate disaster loomed close in the early days of the fighting. Paris was saved from capture and France from defeat not by astute generalship but by the resolute resistance of the French *poilus* and their British allies who fought with an élan not to be shown in World War II. The cost of the victory was the sacrifice of 1,350,000 lives. Victory came only with the arrival of a million-and-a-half American soldiers and the collapse of the German Kaiser's government.

In the interim between the two world wars France, like Britain, shrank from any confrontation that promised a repetition of the suffering. But France found its former allies, Britain and the United States, unwilling to cripple Germany permanently and inclined to support its economic recovery, for now it was under republican government. France recovered Alsace and Lorraine, and modest occupation forces were kept in the German Rhineland until 1930. Nevertheless, France's efforts to recover reparation payments from the Weimar Republic were not supported sympathetically by the British and Americans. Its search for alliances with new states to Germany's east provided small comfort. In its search for security, a stodgy and unimaginative military leadership spent millions of francs preparing for a repetition of World War I. The only expenditures for modern defense systems were those for the extravagant fortifications of the Maginot Line, which never covered the northern border of the state. The central command of the French armies was close to Paris, where it could exercise political influence, but it had no efficient way to communicate with the armies on the frontier. Unlike the Germans, the French had not altered strategy to take into account the new developments in air and tank warfare.

POLITICAL AND ECONOMIC CHAOS

Meanwhile, the French political scene became ever more chaotic. The Bolshevik revolution had created deep reverberations in France. The country's industrial system had never moved much beyond a primitive stage of capitalism, and entrepreneurs often combined antiquated work methods and factory organization with harsh treatment of workers. The Soviet example, despite all its shortcomings and failures, still appealed to workers who had little power to negotiate for better wages and working conditions. As a consequence communism and socialism accumulated much political strength throughout the interwar period. The French Communist party commanded a significant bloc of loyal voters and a large portion of labor union membership. The more moderate Socialist and Radical Socialist (both actually neither radical nor fully socialist) parties also gained votes and labor support. The conservative parties represented those who controlled capital in France, who claimed that only they were able to stabilize the French franc when runaway inflation threatened and keep the factories operating during a period of worldwide depression in the 1930s. And in that period of economic malaise, many Frenchmen were far more concerned with the dangers of Soviet communism's influence than they were with the rise of Mussolini's Fascism and Hitler's Nazism.

Indeed, movements on the right gained considerable support. Royalist sentiment persisted in the League of French Action, whose members, known as the *Camelots du Roi* (King's Peddlers) were always available for right-wing demonstrations. They were joined by Colonel François de la Rocque's *Croix de Feu* (Cross of Fire), originally a war veterans' organization but later enrolling many non-veterans. Italian Fascism itself clearly found much admiration in France. Among the indigenous fascist groups were the organization of French Solidarity, sponsored by the perfume maker François Coty, the Young Patriots of Pierre Taitinger, the *Cagoulards* (Hooded Ones), supported in the ranks of the French army and funded by Mussolini, and the outright fascist league of *Francistes* formed by Marcel Bucard.

By the middle 1930s France was severely divided between right-wing forces opposed to basic economic reforms and the Communist and socialist parties whose membership had burgeoned during the period of economic depression. Specifically, debate raged over the demands of labor unions for better pay and more reasonable working conditions. A so-called popular front government of Communists, Socialists, and Radical Socialists was formed in 1936, and a Socialist premier, Léon Blum (the first Jewish premier during the Third French Republic) was able to obtain some labor reforms. In the same year a mutual assistance pact between France and the Soviet Union was finally ratified, raising the prospect that in a new war Germany would confront foes both on the east and the west. But the pact stirred little support at home, and Germany used it as an excuse for beginning the fortification of its western frontiers. France's only response was ineffective protest. And in that same period the outbreak of the Spanish Civil War between fascist and Spanish popular front forces (which were increasingly influenced by Communist elements as the war progressed) alarmed conservative Frenchmen, especially since the anti-Franco forces had obtained their arms directly from the Soviet Union. The French popular front dissolved, giving way to more conservative and less dynamic leadership. Right-wing groups strengthened themselves during 1938 and 1939 by playing on fears of left-wing extremism, particularly French communism.

MILITARY INCOMPETENCE AND
DISASTROUS DEFEAT

The instability of French political leadership contrasted with the stolid complacency of the French military. The whole decade of the 1930s was dominated by the lackluster leadership of Maurice Gamelin, who became chief of the general staff in 1931 and commander-in-chief of the French army after 1935. Apparently neither he nor many of his subordinates paid much attention to military developments in Germany and Italy, except to decide that France could not challenge them without a full mobilization of its own armies and the aid of the British. The network of command remained primitive; Gamelin's headquarters in Vincennes had no radio, telephone, telegraph, or even carrier-pigeon communication with General Alphonse Georges at La Fertesous-Jouaire, thirty-five miles to the east, or with the Grand General Headquarters, which lay halfway between these two command posts!

France and Great Britain had both remained relatively passive while German forces invaded Poland and destroyed its armies in rapid armored drives. French hopes for generous assistance from the British were disappointed; the Chamberlain government was more interested in securing a land base in Norway than in strengthening French defenses. Still, the British Expeditionary Army of some ten divisions was sent to France. Churchill suggested that the French conduct air strikes against the Germans, but this idea was rebuffed because of the fear of retaliation. A relatively long and deceptively calm period of "Sitzkrieg" followed as neither German nor French and British forces showed any desire for conflict. But when that quiet was broken by the Blitzkrieg on May 10, 1940, the consequences were catastrophic. The Netherlands was overwhelmed by German forces in five days. Belgium had remained neutral, and the French had expected to come to that country's aid when the Germans attacked. The French were subsequently astonished at how rapidly the German forces rolled through Belgium and into lightly defended Ardennes Forest, this after crimping Belgian defenses to the north. The fatal confusion of French leadership was reflected in its feeble response to the brilliant German tactics and the rapid defeat which followed. Postwar studies indicated that hundreds of new French planes were never used in the battle; moreover, France's tank divisions were superior in quality and enjoyed approximate parity with its foe, but this advantage was neutralized by the military's lack of competence in the formation and deployment of armored divisions.

The evacuation of British and French troops from Dunkirk was a miracle of British determination not much applauded by the French; the battle for France that followed from June 5 to June 25, 1940, was marked by the disintegration of the French military and the disgraceful flight of (and dissension within) the government. Although the French endeavored to attribute the disastrous defeat suffered by their country to the failure of the British to give full support, France's political weakness was a more likely cause during that time of crisis, as was the fatuous and incredibly faulty military leadership. Gamelin demonstrated a complete inability to react to the unexpected and novel tactics of the Blitzkrieg. Subordinate generals proved even more inept, and some of them completely lost their nerve in the face of disaster. Premier Paul Reynaud, too much under the influence of his mistress, Helène des Portes, waited far too long to replace Gamelin and then chose another aged and, as events demonstrated, incompetent general, Maxime Weygand. A despairing Reynaud pled with the British to harass the German troops from the air and directed radio appeals to the United States, begging Americans to fill the skies "with clouds of planes." This gesture was utterly ridiculous in a time of American isolationism and military unpreparedness.

German victory was gained in less than two weeks of actual fighting. On June 11 Paris had been declared an open city to spare it from destruction, while the government moved south to Bordeaux in a chaotic and disorganized flight of government officials, businessmen, and their families. In Bordeaux the ministers and the military engaged in disgraceful discussions as to who should issue the order to stop fighting. Weygand insisted that capitulation be shouldered by the civilian authorities so that the honor of the army would not be lost. He indicated furthermore that he would not honor orders of the civilian authorities for a cease-fire and made it quite clear that he had no respect for the democratic government of the Third Republic or for the politicians who represented it. For his part Reynaud could not bring up the courage to relocate the cabinet to France's overseas dominions and continue the war from abroad. When last-ditch efforts to gain greater help from Britain and the United States failed, Reynaud on the night of June 16 stepped down without opting to take up Churchill's hasty offer of a political union with Great Britain, without ordering the navy to turn its ships over to France's ally, and even without obtaining the consent of his own cabinet members before resigning. Albert Lebrun, the president of the Third French Republic, accepted the resignation of Reynaud without consulting the other ministers and named in his place Marshal Henri Pétain, who had entered the French cabinet shortly before the outbreak of war, believing that he had been recalled from his ambassadorship in Spain to save France from "thirty years of Marxism." Since General Weygand insisted that requesting a cease-fire was contrary to the honor of the French army, Pétain obtained surrender terms from the Germans. The victors provided these terms on June 21 in the railroad car that had been the scene of German surrender in World War I. The armistice was concluded on June 25.

Churchill, fearing that the Germans might seize the French navy, ordered "Operation Catapult." On July 3 French naval ships in British ports were taken over and neutralized. The French ships in the Algerian naval base at Mers-el-Kebir at Oran refused to surrender, forcing the British to scuttle most of the French vessels. (The Germans exploited this incident to cool French sentiments for their allies.) Whether or not the British strike was necessary is debatable. Admiral Darlan, commander of the French fleet and not an entirely reliable personality, said the ships would have been scuttled voluntarily or taken to the U.S. even if the British had not acted.

It is difficult to determine the reaction of French civilians to this sudden and "strange defeat" (as the French historian, Marc Bloch, labeled it). Their fear of German bombing was certainly justified by their country's lack of antiaircraft defenses. Worse, civilians had hampered the retreat of the French forces in their efforts to find refuge from the bombs and shells. Photographs from this time show the lines of refugees travelling on bicycles, horses, or on foot as they sought to find some kind of shelter. Thousands whose homes had been destroyed inhabited churches and other public buildings. In the United States, the first strong display of popular support for France came with the newsreel photographs of German dive bombers strafing innocent civilians. If the French had defended Paris, as Churchill had suggested, popular sympathy might have weakened much earlier the potency of isolationist sentiments. But unlike the British, the French populace did not witness heroic battles in the skies over their cities—many French fighters had remained at air schools even after the outbreak of war. There were no inspired last-stand defenses. More than the war had been lost. French honor and pride had been muddied by discordant politics and inept military leadership. In these days of shame and despair, Pétain must have seemed to many Frenchmen like a beacon of hope, a symbol that something still French could be preserved in a time of utter disaster.

Pétain concluded the armistice with the Germans by which France was divided into two parts—two-thirds of the country, including the whole Atlantic coastline and the capital at Paris to be occupied by the Germans, the remaining portion to be governed from a former spa and mineral water resort at Vichy. Pétain had been remembered chiefly for the slogan he had issued at the Battle of Verdun in World War I—"they shall not pass." But neither in that war nor in France's fighting with the Riff in Morocco in 1925 did Pétain demonstrate enlightened military leadership. In all the military discussions that had preceded World War II, Pétain championed the building of the Maginot Line and of static, mass defense on remaining unprotected sections of the French frontier. Strongly rightist in politics, his name had been linked with some of the parafascist leagues before the war. His personal assumption of power after the armistice was characterized by the same authoritarian traits that Hitler and Mussolini displayed.

The armistice that Pétain signed with the Germans on June 22, 1940, left a million-and-a-half French prisoners of war in German hands; most of them would remain incarcerated until 1945. The surrender provided only that French navy ships be gathered up in French ports and disarmed (which did not assure the British that the Germans might not later ready them for action) and that all military action in the French empire as well as in France itself end.

THE NATURE OF THE VICHY REGIME

In his mid-eighties and partly senile, Pétain seemed to relish his new-found power. He addressed the nation as "We, Pétain," a throwback to monarchism, and allowed a cult of personality with special songs and prayers to flourish. Assuming the title of Chief of the French State, Pétain claimed complete executive and legislative power, excepting the declaration of war. Through most of the history of Vichy he was closely associated with Pierre Laval, who was named Pétain's successor (he was later replaced by Admiral Darlan and then restored to power again). All civil servants and soldiers were required to take an oath of personal obedience to Pétain.

The keynote of the regime was a return to the old values of France—"family, work, and patriotism" replaced the revolutionary slogan of "liberty, equality, and fraternity." The family allowance, a subsidy designed to encourage larger families and discourage working mothers, was increased, but its effect was quickly reduced by the onset of inflation. Divorce became more difficult, adoption easier, and abortion prohibited. The influence of labor unions was destroyed, and business was largely controlled by associations of employers. The church regained its long-lost dominance over personal lives. School teachers and professors with left-wing leanings were purged, and camps for younger men sprang up to provide indoctrination and supply labor in the countryside. Girls received more physical, vocational, and domestic instruction than they had under the Republic.

The popular reaction to these changes is difficult to judge. Certainly there was some sentiment that Pétain's regime had at least preserved some semblance of an independent France. But the costs of this independence included a wide-reaching purge of political opponents or those suspected of opposition. Foreigners, socialists, democrats, and Masons found themselves disqualified for any kind of public employment. Some naturalized foreigners were "denaturalized." And Vichy shared in the implementation of German anti-Semitic policies. Early on the Vichy regime voluntarily adopted laws restricting Jewish activity in government, the press, banking, and real estate and outlawing Jewish ownership of businesses employing Aryans. Jews were to constitute no more than 2 percent of all lawyers and doctors and no more than 3 percent of university students. Vichy adopted these harsh measures voluntarily. More severe restrictions came later under German pressure.

Undoubtedly the great majority of people in unoccupied France simply accepted the status quo with quiet resignation. Many were pleased that the "irreligious" and left-wing Third Republic had been replaced with a more conservative government. Others thought that France could be freed only with help from abroad; for the moment there was nothing to do but "wait" for that liberation. These "waiters" (*attentistes*) probably were the most numerous portion of the Vichy population. They were preoccupied with the search for survival. The Germans set a high exchange rate for the German mark against French francs. This allowed them to buy up the remaining stocks of merchandise in the stores and to eat at restaurants that quickly became too expensive for most Frenchmen. Vichy families depended on secure jobs and wages. Many hoped for the return of husbands and sons who were prisoners of war in German camps. Shortages of food and fuel caused great hardship in Vichy, as they did in Paris, and tuberculosis increased. Still, opposition to the regime was muted. If the resistance movement in France began as an "infinitesimal minority" of its citizens, that statement was particularly true of Vichy more than the rest of occupied France.

Indeed, many citizens of Vichy were *collabos*, sympathetic with Nazi Germany and its principles. Pierre Laval personified this attitude, although his personal ambition probably was as important as his political principles. He was Pétain's chief advisor from July to December 1940, but was succeeded by Pierre Étienne Flandin and then by Admiral Jean Darlan until restored to power in April 1942. He would retain his second-in-command status until the end of the Vichy regime in August 1944. Nevertheless, the extent of Vichy's collaboration with Nazi Germany did not depend greatly on who was in power. Local officials were confronted with the choice of following German guidelines or losing their posts. Most collaborated. After January 1943 the Vichy regime created a kind of military police, the *Milice*, to combat growing opposition. In many respects the methods of the *Milice* resembled those of the Gestapo.

THE GERMAN OCCUPATION

Meanwhile, more than two-thirds of the country had come under direct German administration since the armistice. The two northern coastal departments of France, Nord and Pas-de-Calais, were placed under the military jurisdiction of the German field commander in Belgium, who set up headquarters at Lille. Although the Germans insisted that this arrangement was simply an administrative decision, the French protested (to no avail), feeling that it portended a permanent separation of these departments from the home country. The Germans responded that the area concerned needed to be unified to facilitate the defense of the Continent against the British, but few Frenchmen believed this explanation.

The historically disputed provinces of Alsace and Lorraine were dealt with separately. After some delay, they were simply incorporated into Germany—Alsace joined the administration of Baden under *Gauleiter* Robert Wagner while Lorraine and the Saar became a part of the Saar-Pfalz Gau under Josef Bürckel. This disposition was strongly protested by French negotiators as a violation of armistice conditions. (Germany's process of separating and annexing these French territories was kept secret for several years.) In 1940 Bürckel announced plans to relocate 100,000 French sympathizers from the "Germanized" Lorraine back to France. In spite of protests from Vichy and see-saw negotiations, some 58,000 were transported.

The remaining areas of occupied France fell under the command of General Walther von Brauchitsch. The details of this administration were, however, much confused during the initial period of occupation. Otto Abetz, a representative of the German Foreign Office, received support from Hitler, but so did an armistice committee that met in Wiesbaden. To those who have studied the overlapping and confusing administrative order in

Germany itself, the competition of agencies all vying for control of defeated France is not surprising.

Paris was the military headquarters for occupied France (excepting departments supervised from Lille). The first military commander was an older professional general, Alfred Streccius, who presided from his headquarters in the Hotel Majestic. During his term the idea of moving the French administration at Vichy back to Paris was considered but did not eventuate in action. The relatively quiet administration of Streccius ended on October 31, 1940, when he was replaced by General Otto von Stülpnagel, the first of two cousins with the same last name who held command in Paris.

The German troops had been told to behave "correctly" in Paris, and some Parisians found them more acceptable than the G.I.'s who arrived later. But their presence was obvious throughout the city. The names of some streets were changed for the Germans' convenience; the whole quarter of Avenue Kleber was shut off for their usage. The occupiers also set aside the railroad station at St. Lazaire for official business. The Theater of the Empire, like many others in the city, was made to serve the needs of German soldiers, and the German slogan *Kraft durch Freude*, used by the Nazi entertainment organization, was placed above its doors. German officers appropriated apartments and furnished them luxuriously with the prized possessions of Parisians—including works of art and other cherished objects. The favorable exchange rate of francs to marks allowed German soldiers to buy up the goods civilians found more difficult to obtain. Although most Parisians accepted the presence of the soldiers as an unavoidable evil, under the surface there was a deep resentment of the conquerors.

Similar occupation arrangements governed Nantes, Bordeaux, and other French cities. Alongside the military commanders and actually operating to a considerable degree independently of them were the forces of the *Sicherheitsdienst*. In Paris Karl Albrecht Oberg oversaw this organization. Oberg had had a long period of service with the SS and the SD. A protégé of Reinhard Heydrich, infamous for his treatment of Czechoslovakia, Oberg employed his own brand of cruelty. In Paris Oberg was designated the direct personal representative of Heinrich Himmler and was given authority to function in his behalf in relations with Stülpnagel, von Rundstedt, Ambassador Abetz, and the French government. Himmler was, of course, anticipating a postwar period in which the SS would absorb the military, leaving him and his representatives totally responsible for keeping security and quiet throughout German-held territories. Although Oberg had a relatively minimal number of German police under his direct control, he directed also the French police and exercised preventive action against cells of opposition.

The area under direct German occupation had contained the more liberal regions of prewar France including Communist and socialist groups of the factory workers and left-of-center writers and teachers. Here early resistance to Nazism took the form of helping escaped French prisoners of war find refuge in the south or in England. Other groups organized to produce illegal newspapers encouraging opposition to the regime. In these activities many French women carried out roles more dangerous than those of their male counterparts, working at night in secret press offices and smuggling newspapers for delivery in their shopping bags. Many of them paid for these actions with their lives. There also began relatively numerous cases of retaliatory violence against German forces. Individual *Franc-Tireurs* gunned down lone soldiers or officers.

HOSTAGES AND FORCED LABOR

Late in October 1941 the field commander in Nantes was shot to death, and the next day a counselor for the military administration in Bordeaux was murdered. The procedure well established in Russia was prescribed for France. For each death, fifty hostages were ordered shot. Authorities offered a large reward for the discovery of the perpetrator. Stülpnagel followed directions in spite of some reservations, and forty-eight Communists and Jews under arrest were shot in Nantes and fifty in Bordeaux. Still bombings and shootings continued, and Stülpnagel began to regard the killing of hostages as not only ineffective but also as contrary to his soldierly honor. Claiming illness, he resigned from his post, indicating privately that he could not allow the demands for new victims. Whether his soldierly honor or personal resentment at orders emanating from the rival SS was more critical to his decision remains uncertain. His replacement, in a sort of ironic turnabout, was his cousin Karl Heinrich Stülpnagel, who followed directives without qualms until the closing days of German occupation brought him, too, into conflict with the Gestapo. Implicated in the plot of German officers to assassinate Hitler in 1944, Karl Stülpnagel tried to commit suicide but failed. Half-dead, he was carried to Plötzensee prison in Berlin. His successor, the last German military governor of Paris, was Major General Dietrich von Cholitz, infamous for his brutality against Rotterdam and Sebastopol.

Perhaps the most seriously resented action of the German authorities was the conscription of hundreds of thousands of Frenchmen into forced labor battalions in Germany. In the earlier months of occupation, some Frenchmen had volunteered for this service in the expectation that this would bring the release and repatriation of French soldiers held as prisoners of war. This did not occur. The German authorities did allow some visits, released sick soldiers, and granted minor accommodations for family problems, but well over a million French soldiers remained in Germany working on the farms or in munitions plants. Some 185,000 French workers voluntarily flowed into Germany. But in the spring of 1942, Fritz Sauckel, the German labor chief, sought an additional 250,000 workers. Before Sauckel's action was completed, some 600,000 French men and women had joined the million French prisoners of war working on German farms or in war industries.

French factories also produced materiel for the German war effort. Somua produced cars, and Citroen and Renault produced trucks "for the king of Prussia," as a popular saying went. But shops and businesses not vital to the war effort found no choice but to close their doors. Luxury hotels stayed afloat with German patronage, lesser ones fell on hard times. The Allies bombed French industries as the war went on, but these raids never produced the degree of destruction visited upon German cities.

Many small-scale French factories and workshops saw first a decline in their production of non-military materials, then a complete stoppage in many cases. The British blockade against the Continent was undoubtedly more effective in crippling France than other countries further inland. Records in Paris indicate that the receipt of goods declined to less than one-sixth of prewar levels between 1939 and 1944. Bombing hampered also the reception of foodstuffs, ironically making rationing for French civilians more difficult. Always handed out first to German soldiers, food supplies sank to miserable levels during the war. By 1944 the rations in France were lower than anywhere else on the Continent.

THE GREAT MISERY OF PARIS

The city of lights was filled with great misery during the war. Shortages of food, clothing, drugs, and hospital supplies, the cold of the long winters with little heat, and the difficulties of traversing a city where in 1944 only 500 automobiles (as against 350,000 before the war) and 166 buses operated, affected all Parisians. Overworked metro trains carried immense loads; during bombardments they parked in the tunnels as the air grew fetid for the jammed-on occupants. Some bicycles were pushed into service to provide transport to work, but their value escalated inordinately during the war, passing the prewar prices of automobiles. Workers housed their bicycles in garages during the day at work and at night kept them in the safe interiors of their apartments. High prices and low salaries added to a dark and meager daily existence.

The physical darkness of the German occupation was overshadowed by the spiritual blackness. German authorities required the registration of all Jews in France in 1940. For thousands of Jewish refugees from Germany and other parts of Europe, their hard-won escape from danger was imperilled again. Some fled across the frontier to Spain, but this fascist state soon closed its borders to this traffic. French authorities sought to separate those Jews who were French citizens from the mass of refugees. Other Jews in the occupied zone found themselves prisoners, serving as hostages for the punishment of anti-German actions.

The darkest days of occupation came after June 1942 when the German authorities ordered that the Vichy regime turn over all non-French Jews within the unoccupied territory. By that time the evacuation of foreign Jews from the occupied area to eastern Europe was well underway. Tens of thousands more were now added to those numbers by the Vichy government. Regular army and SS troops moved these Jews across the countryside in trucks and boxcars without food, water, sanitary facilities, or access to medical care. One of the most grievous events was the penning of some 15,000 Jews in the sport palace (*Vélodrome d'Hiver*) in Paris in cramped, unclean quarters lacking both food and water. Thousands of children were separated from their parents and died in solitary misery. In one of the ironies of the war, some Jews residing in France were able to survive by taking refuge in the Italian zone of occupation in southeastern France, where officials were lax in enforcing anti-Semitic measures. Many Jews eventually made their way into Italy proper.

To its credit, the Vichy regime had resisted the demands for the delivery of French Jews, still considering them to be French citizens. Some courageous people also protected and harbored foreign Jews in some parts of Vichy France. But France, known as a political and social refuge before the war, lost much of that reputation during this period. The number of Jews who were shipped to the concentration camp at Drancy and then on to the extermination camps in Poland is not entirely certain— estimates vary from 75,000 to 90,000.

THE RESISTANCE

On June 18, 1940, Charles de Gaulle, who had gone to London on the eve of the French surrender, made a radio appeal in which he proclaimed his determination to continue the war from abroad. De Gaulle called upon all French military and naval officers abroad to rally to his call. Although he had in the 1930s been a vocal critic of the outmoded tactical thinking of the French military command, he was not well known either inside or outside of France. His disputes with superiors over the importance of armored warfare had been kept within the military establishment.

He had remained a colonel during the first days of the German offensive in May 1940, and his relatively minor exploits during his command of the Fourth Armored Division escaped widespread notice. All of France's stodgy military leaders disliked him. Two weeks into the German campaign, de Gaulle was promoted to brigadier general. As France's military defeat neared, de Gaulle called for the creation of resistance forces. He added to that request the requirement that those signing up for his Free French forces had to pledge loyalty to his person. Like Pétain, he used the plural *nous* (we) in his official statements. Winston Churchill accepted his claim to leadership but was always to find dealing with him troublesome. De Gaulle was, he said, a cross between Joan of Arc and Jesus Christ. The Americans, who maintained touchy diplomatic relations with Vichy France, were to maintain serious reservations about de Gaulle's leadership until well after the invasion of France.

To citizens in occupied France, de Gaulle was for some time a little-known entity. Few of them heard the famous radio broadcast from Great Britain. In Vichy France more placed their hope in Pétain, who it was thought might moderate German demands. In occupied France there was considerable concern that de Gaulle's right-wing sympathies might cause him to ignore or limit the contributions of Communists and socialists.

The extent of "resistance" in France remains somewhat cloudy, even in the best works on the subject. One must recall that the occupying forces and their collaborators could wield frightening methods to discourage opposition. It was not just that one risked death by opposing the Germans. The French knew of the cruelty the Nazi regime exercised in Germany and quickly deduced that those arrested in France undoubtedly faced torture before death. Too often that arrest was the handiwork of an informer posing as a member of the resistance while serving in the pay of Vichy or German police agencies. It took a special bravery to contemplate any action that contradicted the orders of the German authorities. In any society that kind of bravery is restricted to a very small segment of the population.

Early defiance of the harsh German occupation was carried on largely by small and uncoordinated groups with limited objectives: getting Allied soldiers to places of safety in England or through southern France into Spain; helping British (and later American) agents to gather intelligence on German fortifications and armaments; or just painting anti-German slogans on fences at night. In these early activities women played a notable part, and numbers of them paid for their actions with torture and death. One of the earliest public manifestations of resistance came on November 11, 1940, the anniversary of the armistice of World War I. Several thousand students assembled at the Arc de Triomphe to lay flowers at the tomb of the Unknown Soldier. When they began to sing the "Marseillaise," they were fired upon and beaten. The Germans closed the University of Paris for the remainder of the semester.

New resistance organizations often sprang up without central planning or direction. Hatred of the Germans, opposition to the stodginess and narrow-mindedness of the Vichy regime, memories of prewar ideals of freedom and working-class solidarity, and a stubborn refusal to accept the consequences of military defeat characterized these groups. Liberal Catholic groups in and around the city of Lyons coalesced in the organization *Combat*. This underground agency was the work of Henri Frenay, a young captain in the French army who had been captured in northern France but escaped and worked his way south into unoccupied France. Frenay sought aid from military leaders in Vichy but got a cold shoulder. Thus Frenay shaped his resistance group largely by his own efforts. His procedure involved recruiting various "national" leaders who had to build up their own cadres of workers. This process always involved the danger of taking into the ranks a *collabo* who would reveal the group's existence to the police. Although Frenay hoped to establish a secret army, the numbers of this resistance militia grew slowly until the end of 1942. Moreover, some factions of the group, such as those formed by law professor François de Menthon, did not want to employ physical violence against collaborators. *Combat* was to claim 70,000 to 75,000 followers by the end of 1942.

Two other resistance groups in southern France were more open to socialist and left-wing groups than *Combat*. One of these was *Libération*, led by Emmanuel d'Astier de la Vigerie, a journalist. The other was *Franc-Tireur*, formed by Jean-Pierre Lévy, a Jewish entrepeneur. This last group was more openly and outspokenly opposed to Pétain's government than the other two. Although these three groups opposed the Germans, they remained suspicious of one another through much of the period that followed.

The Communist-dominated *Front National* operated in both Vichy and occupied France, although its greatest strength naturally was in the north. As has been seen, the Communists shared with Jews the dubious honor of being the first victims of German reprisals, both groups providing ready hostages to be executed whenever resistance fighters caused German casualties. Their past history of oppression and action under hostile conditions made it easier for them to assume the perils of resistance, unlike the quiescent middle-class and intellectual cadres of the other resistance groups.

DE GAULLE'S MOVE TO LEADERSHIP

De Gaulle realized that the existence of varying and competing groups within France imperilled his own ambitions to establish personal authority when France was liberated. On January 1, 1942, he made his first direct contact with resistance groups when he sent Jean Moulin into France as his personal representative. Moulin had been the prefect at Chartres in May 1940 and was tortured by the Germans for refusing to blame black colonial soldiers for the deaths of French civilians actually caused by bombardments. He was dismissed from office by Vichy but became aware of the burgeoning resistance movements. Moulin managed to get to London and convinced de Gaulle that the general needed to bring these movements under his leadership. Descending by parachute into France to meet with the leaders of *Combat, Libération*, and *Franc-Tireur*, he was able to get those groups to join in the Unified Movements of Resistance (*Mouvements Unis de la Résistance*) by March 1943. He was, of course, aided in this accomplishment by de Gaulle's provision of considerable monetary subsidies for the work of the resistance.

Although the resistance groups in France recognized that de Gaulle possessed British aid and sympathy, those on the left were concerned about his long-range objectives. Christian Pineau, a leader of the resistance group *Libération-Nord*, visited de Gaulle in London and returned with the general's assurance that post-war France would have a democratic government and social security. The resistance groups adopted his cause and rejected the American-sponsored General Henri Giraud, who had been chosen to lead French forces in North Africa. Still, they resented the efforts of some of de Gaulle's agents to direct decisions of the resistance organizations. De Gaulle, for his part, wanted to be sure that when liberation came the "secret army" would be under his own control. In spite of the declaration of allegiance from Communist resistance groups, de Gaulle never fully trusted them. But Léon Blum, the elder statesman of the Socialist party in France and leader of the popular front in the 1930s, pronounced his support for de Gaulle in October 1942.

In spite of some controversy between resisters and de Gaulle, his leadership remained fairly secure until the capture of Jean Moulin at Caluire on June 21, 1943. Moulin died about a month later, enduring terrible tortures at the hands of the Gestapo. (Involved in this torture was the infamous Klaus Barbie, the head of the Gestapo in Lyons, whose "interrogation" of Moulin was responsible for his death.) Moulin was the most celebrated hero of the resistance, and his death left the lines of communication between de Gaulle and the underground movements less secure than they had been. De Gaulle remained fearful that Communist and left-wing groups would resist his leadership when liberation came.

Hindering the coordination of resistance groups in France were the contrary actions of intelligence organizations, first the British and later the American. The British Special Operations Executive (S.O.E.) worked separately from the British secret intelligence service (SIS or MI6). Later the Americans set up the Office of Strategic Services (OSS), which worked in cooperation with the British agencies. The operations of these agencies, however, were not fully integrated until January 1944. All three groups provided funds to help French resistance organizations and activities, but their effectiveness was blunted by the contrasting demands and mutual suspicion that the resistance organizations had for each other. For their part, French resisters were not always confident of the motives and methods of these intelligence groups.

THE REMAINDER OF FRANCE OCCUPIED

On May 29, 1942, German forces occupied all of France in response to the invasion of North Africa. Hitler said the treachery of French officers in North Africa had nullified the treaty arrangements. With this action, any feeling that Vichy had saved France from complete German control was lost. Although Pétain protested, German troops pushed all the way through southern France. Laval replaced Pétain as chief of the government in Vichy and was handed the power to issue personal decrees and choose ministers. In this last phase of his leadership, Laval hoped to moderate the severity of German occupation by continuing to cooperate, even though he knew he faced execution if Germany were defeated.

The German occupation of the south was followed on November 27, 1942, by *Unternehmen Attila*, in which powerful armored columns moved to take over the port of Toulon. There the remnants of the French navy had been brought together after being pursued by a British fleet intending to prevent the ships from being refitted by the Germans. Three submarines escaped to Algiers; the rest of the fleet in Toulon was scuttled by French personnel. The Germans kept this action secret from even the Italians, and Pétain was not informed of these plans until the action was already underway.

The occupation of Vichy France was accompanied by a new demand from the German labor chief, Fritz Sauckel, for 250,000 additional workers from France (to join the 932,000 already there). Sauckel's demands swelled the ranks of *Maquisards* in southern France, those who sought to escape the labor draft by taking refuge in the nearby forest brush. There they created bands of poorly armed resisters who harassed German soldiers and French *milices*. Although these irregular forces vexed the Germans, they were always short of food and lacking the up-to-date weaponry needed to inflict serious harm on the enemy. They claimed that the British never provided the kind of support they deserved, but given the constant menace of German planes and the visibility of parachute drops to enemy troops, the charges have little substance. Providing any assistance was extremely difficult.

After 1942, German forces governed with a sense of desperation. On a number of occasions all civilized standards were discarded. At times the Germans forced the cooperative *milice* to
carry out ruthless deeds. At other times they acted on their own.
On January 4, 1943, a bomb blast at a casino in Marseilles killed
a number of German soldiers and injured others. The occupation authorities demanded that the French police clear out this
"pigsty" by levying fines and clearing out sections of the city
that harbored known anti-German groups. This action was carried out on January 24, and although the French action may have
been less punitive than if the Germans themselves had carried it
out, it was clear that the last remnant of independent French
rule had been destroyed. Similarly the Germans claimed that an
attack on their garrison at Tulle on June 7, 1944, was accompanied by the pitiless killing of several soldiers; they responded by
hanging some 120 supposed *Maquisards*.

Two later events even more vividly underscored the vicious-
ness of Nazi occupation. On June 10, 1944, German troops invested the little village of Oradour-sur-Glane, killing all the
villagers, including women and children of all ages, and burning
every house. An estimated 700 inhabitants lost their lives. In the
aftermath of the story it emerged that the German patrol had
been directed to liquidate the village of Oradour-sur-Vayres,
where explosives had supposedly been found, but the Germans'
poor command of geography led them to destroy the wrong village. Another tiny village, Marsoulas, was wiped out and all its
inhabitants killed on June 13, 1944—seven men, six women, and
fourteen children, including an eighteen-month-old baby.

THE FIGHTING FRENCH

In the last years of the war, the number of French resisters involved in military action and sabotage increased greatly. The
French Forces of the Interior (FFI) grew significantly and received larger quantities of arms and explosives. It is estimated
that altogether 200,000 were enrolled. But their efforts were often accompanied by misunderstandings and tragedy. On June 13,
1944, some 3,500 poorly armed *Maquisards* occupied a plateau at
Vercors between the valleys of the Rhone and the Isère rivers.

Around them were some 20,000 German troops with overwhelming firepower. Expecting a landing of Allied troops bearing arms and supplies, the *Maquisards* prepared an airstrip. But landing instead were 500 crack SS troops, who used their vantage to augment the artillery fire pouring in from below. In the ensuing struggle practically all of the *Maquisards* were killed.

Allied leaders did give credit to the FFI for its activities before and after the Normandy invasion began. French resistance forces provided precise information about the disposition of German forces in Normandy, including a detailed, fifty-foot-long map that pinpointed the size and location of German units in the vicinity. French peasants had also persuaded some German officers not to mine areas where they were gardening, making Allied advances less precarious. And French forces harried three major German SS divisions, delaying their arrival in the invasion area. In the twenty-four hours after D-Day 180 German trains were derailed and some 500 railway lines cut. Resistance forces also disrupted communications and destroyed mine fields. Eisenhower was later to say that their activities had shortened the campaign by two months.

As the Allied armies moved into France, a serious debate broke out over the role to be played by Charles de Gaulle. The Americans had retreated from earlier efforts to replace the flamboyant and egotistical Free French leader. But they had also discovered that the French resented greatly any bombing of French cities, even ones invested by German troops. Therefore, the Americans determined initially that the invasion forces would bypass Paris, hoping that it could be cut off and left to "die on the vine." Those who had planned the invasion had pointed out that efforts to take the city would result in considerable casualties. Moreover, supplies would be depleted by the heavy consumption of gasoline needed to move troops into the city and by the enormous demand for food and basic necessities needed by Paris's population, which was close to starvation by this time.

But to leave Paris to its own fate carried with it the danger that the Communist resistance forces, which were strong in the city, might rise and carry out a successful takeover. If they were able to establish a new government there de Gaulle realized that his claims to leadership would be jeopardized. Consequently, he secured from Eisenhower permission (it seems that he would have acted without this permission had it not been given) to detach General Jacques Philippe Leclerc's Second Armored Division to move against Paris. Resistance groups within the city rose against the Germans on August 17, 1944, and Leclerc's forces, accompanied by the U.S. Fourth Infantry Division, arrived in Paris on August 24. In that interim between the rising of the Paris resistance groups and the arrival of Leclerc's forces, General Dietrich von Cholitz ensured the salvation of the city from the usual destruction visited on places evacuated by the Germans. Von Cholitz countermanded Hitler's orders to carry out the destruction of Paris's monuments and artistic treasures. The last commander of the city, like his two predecessors, the Stülpnagels, had revealed a soft spot in his Prussian armor.

On August 25, 1944, de Gaulle arrived in Paris to assume direction of the government of France. Paris, he said on that occasion, had been "liberated by itself, by its own people, with the help of the armies of France..." There was no mention of the other armies that had fought to establish the landings in Normandy and that would bear the brunt of the remainder of the conflict with Germany. The demonstration of support de Gaulle received from the populace provided a clear indication that he was the only figure capable of directing the return to republican government.

In the aftermath of France's liberation there were numerous incidents of vengeance against those who had collaborated with the Germans. Most prominent was Pierre Laval, who was found guilty and executed; Pétain was also found guilty but allowed to live on in disgrace; he died in 1951 at the age of ninety-five. Many lesser persons were also convicted and executed. Certainly some of the *milices* may have deserved the harsh sentences they received. In other cases there was little justification for the retribution exacted. Some 10,000 to 20,000 died in the terror that followed the liberation. In addition 50,000 were arrested, 800 executed, and 20,000 imprisoned. The purging continued long after the war. In January 1953, twenty-one survivors of the *Reich* division of the SS, the unit responsible for the massacre of 642 residents of Oradour-sur-Glane, were brought to trial. Among those tried were Alsatians, Frenchmen who had been made German citizens during the war; they claimed that they had been inducted into the SS against their will. Nevertheless, they received with the rest a sentence of hard labor. Legislative action later freed them, but only after much political discussion.

Some may argue that if one was not a part of the resistance, he or she was a collaborator. But those who can be clearly classified as resisters were always a small minority. Thirty thousand French men, women, and children were executed by the Germans. Another 25,000 were killed in fighting with German or Vichy forces. A third of the 200,000 French deportees who died in Germany were political prisoners. Obviously many more hated the Germans and what they did, hated the Vichy regime and its duplicity, and hated themselves for not having the courage and will to join the resistance. Those who judge others must first judge themselves, but this did not occur in the immediate aftermath of liberation. A lingering shame hampered efforts to confront the implications of Vichy's history. "The Vichy Syndrome," as Henry Rousso was to designate it, affected politics and the French collective memory of World War II for many years after its conclusion. The acclaim for the semi documentary movie *The Sorrow and the Pity* revealed the dark shadows which lay across the wartime history of France. The long delay in seeking the return of Klaus Barbie and the course of his trial in 1985 further disclosed the deep scars that had covered the proud face of France during World War II.

World War II took a terrible toll on the French. Military and civilian war deaths added up to 600,000. But of this sum, only a third died in military action. Bombardments, executions, massacres, and deportations were the major causes of death. Malnutrition, tuberculosis, and infant mortality also claimed a share of victims. And although the Third French Republic was replaced by a "new" Fourth French Republic, the postwar state encountered many of the same divisions and discords that had hampered the prewar state.

Later in his career de Gaulle sought a compromise between complete democracy and a republic with a strong executive. In the process he renewed a wounded French pride and ended a long period of military insecurity. And in his diplomatic negotiations with Konrad Adenauer, the leader of the democratic German Federal Republic, he achieved a treaty that proclaimed the end of centuries of German-French discord. French morale, severely shaken by World War II, was at last restored.

4 / THE AXIS POWERS:

GERMANY AND ITALY

Germany entered World War I expecting a quick victory in a *frisch und fröhlicher Krieg* (a fresh and happy war). It suffered a grievous defeat, in considerable part due to the intervention of the United States on behalf of the Allies. Adolf Hitler learned little from German history. Although he gained popular support by promising to redress Germany's humiliation in the First World War, his leadership in World War II duplicated many of the errors made by imperial Germany.

Weimar Germany had breached several of the military limitations set by the Treaty of Versailles. During the 1920s weaponry was much improved, and the navy produced the "pocket battleships" that frightened Germany's neighbors. The military also experimented with new aircraft types. But Germany was by no means prepared for war when Hitler took over in 1933. Hitler could not acknowledge publicly that he was restoring the army to full strength until 1935, and even then he accepted an initial limitation of that army to 500,000 men. That he then moved four years later to launch full-scale warfare despite the incomplete state of rearmament represented an action as rash as the Kaiser's in 1914. Even more incredible was that Hitler waited until early 1943, almost four years after the beginning of the war, before he called for all-out warfare, "the nation-in-arms" ideal created by the French in 1793. Hitler had a light-hearted (one would also say "light-headed") regard for the demands of modern warfare.

GERMAN MILITARY SPIRIT

Hitler had from the very first appealed to the military spirit and warlike élan of the German people. Even before he came to power, his followers had marched to the sound of drums and trumpets, carrying rows of flags and standards and bearing the mien of military discipline. The Nazi party recruited the young boys and girls for the *Hitler Jugend* (Hitler Youth) and the *Bund deutscher Mädel* (League of German Girls), who drilled so fervently that their feet ached for days afterwards. Pride in Germany's military survived the World War I defeat. Antiwar publications and satires on the German army had not achieved real popularity during the Weimar period. Hitler's re-creation of the German army seemed to indicate that the nation had recovered its lost pride.

Hitler's initial foreign policy successes, accomplished at minimal cost, further elevated his reputation. In 1935 the Saar, made into a separately administered area by the Treaty of Versailles, voted in a plebiscite to return to the Reich. A year later Hitler's new and poorly prepared army became his pawn in the dramatic, high-stakes occupation of the Rhineland, which had been demilitarized by the Treaty of Versailles. France, however, was too divided politically and too ill-prepared militarily to do more than protest.

In 1938 Hitler bullied a weak Austrian government into abandoning its sovereignty, bringing about the *Anschluss* (union) of Germany and Austria. The two German-speaking states had been allied in World War I. Now they became parts of a "Greater Germany," the title portending the direction of Hitler's next moves. The Führer wanted other German-speaking peoples to be "brought home" to the Reich. Among these were the Sudeten Germans, a minority group living along the frontiers of the state of Czechoslovakia created after World War I. The Sudetenland had never been a part of Germany, yet Hitler declared this area to be an integral part of the Reich. With fear and trembling Great Britain and France accepted the partition of Czechoslovakia, now left defenseless against its greedy neighbor.

If Hitler had critics and doubters, their numbers shrank precipitately with these head-turning successes. These "victories" had been won without the shedding of blood, and the resulting confidence discouraged any serious reconsideration of the state of German military preparedness. Troops had marched into Austria and acquired significant capital funds for rearmament. The western powers' reluctance to risk war over Czechoslovakia had been aided by visits to German armament plants by the legendary American pilot Charles Lindbergh and the French general Joseph Vuillemin. Their reports on the status of German military preparedness were based upon officially sponsored inspections and undoubtedly exaggerated the strength of German arms. Upon its takeover of the Sudeten areas, the German military acquired a first-hand look at fortifications similar to those of France's Maginot Line, and it also absorbed a considerable number of good medium-weight Czech tanks. At nearly the same time Hitler selected Fritz Todt, who had been responsible for the building of the *Autobahnen*, the German super-highway system, as supreme coordinator in the construction of the *Westwall* (Siegfried Line) to defend Germany's frontier with France. This effort tended to reduce popular fears of a potential invasion of German territory.

DID THE GERMAN PUBLIC WANT WAR?

"Public opinion" of Hitler's actions is not easy to measure. The Nazi party, which determined the course of everyday life, had grown enormously between 1933 and 1939. The chain of command started with the *Reichsleiter* (National leaders) and then the *Gauleiter* (regional leaders), the *Kreisleiter* (county leaders), the *Ortsgruppenleiter* (city leaders), the *Blockleiter* (block leaders), and finally the *Zellenleiter* (cell leaders). And within each of these administrative divisions were party leaders who specialized in economic affairs, labor problems, agricultural policy, and so on. Ancillary groups included the Hitler Youth, the League of German Girls, various women's organizations, and the SS and SA.

All newspapers, radio broadcasts, movie productions, and public speeches were controlled by the Nazi propaganda chief, Joseph Goebbels. Rumors and secret information sources existed, of course, but it was dangerous even to recount jokes about the regime. Everywhere agents of the *Gestapo* (the state secret police) were present, sometimes openly, sometimes secretly. From all over the country these agents filed reports on the public mood, the so-called *Stimmungsberichte*, which noted reactions to party actions and speeches. Public criticism was not tolerated. Known Communists and many Social Democrats had been the first victims of Nazi terrorism. Other potential critics were closely watched and often served brief prison terms to frighten them into submission. Only the military had some measure of independence from party leadership.

But in spite of party propaganda, it seems clear that the outbreak of war in September 1939 did not generate the kind of public euphoria that had accompanied the events of 1914. There were no great crowds on the streets clamoring for conquest. This was to be "Hitler's War." The easy conquest of Poland, the rapid occupation of Norway and Denmark, and the surprisingly sudden defeat of France came with only modest casualties for the Germans. By June 1940, only Great Britain remained at war. The colorful books depicting these accomplishments sold well in Germany. Soldiers on leave displayed a high morale to civilians. Food rations remained adequate, although some scarcer items found their way to the black market. Polish workers were brought in to assist in farm work, releasing German farmers to serve in the armed forces. Reports on these workers urged close supervision of these unreliable "guest" workers, but few suggested that this enforced labor was immoral or improper. Germans worried about being defiled by "these filthy creatures," but no one suggested that they should be helped to be less filthy. Poles were soon joined by French workers, apparently treated somewhat better, although their supposed sexual adventures caused concern.

The Nazi party also sought to influence common rituals and customs. Marriages were conducted under the swastika, and burials of soldiers were officiated by both military and party officials. The party attempted to weaken religious fidelity. Meetings of party youth groups were scheduled on Sunday to make it difficult for Hitler Youth and League of German Girls members to attend their church activities. The party pursued those members who left the established churches and declared themselves "*Gottgläubige*," believers in God free of the "negative" influence of priests or pastors.

But even in 1940, domestic observers reported that the continued war with Great Britain troubled Germans. The public recalled Britain's stubborn opposition in World War I. The Nazi press sought to alleviate this concern with reports of damage wrought on British shipping by German submarines. The heroism of the Luftwaffe, commanded by World War I ace Hermann Göring, filled the accounts of the raids on English targets. Through the first two years of the war, the Luftwaffe enjoyed a considerable superiority over the R.A.F. But after June, 1940, British bombers, despite their slowness and supposed obsolescence, did reach German cities. Air defenses destroyed or disabled many of the British invaders, and damages and casualties to Germans were minimal, but evidence was growing that subduing the British lion was not going to be easy. The exchange of U.S. destroyers for naval bases in August, 1940, also posed to the Germans the serious possibility that the United States would eventually enter the war.

PROBLEMS WITH THE CHURCHES

The most persistent source of opposition to the regime was the religious establishment. The Nazis had sought to incorporate the Protestant churches into their base of support. A Prussian army chaplain, Ludwig Müller, was named as "Reichsbishop" for the Protestants. Müller's selection was backed by a German Christian movement that had gained considerable support after Hitler came to power. The extremists in this movement were willing to see the whole Old Testament teachings and the gospel of Paul discarded. Some were close to regarding Hitler as a special messenger of God if not God himself. But well-known Protestant leaders Otto Dibelius, Martin Niemöller, Dietrich Bonnhoeffer, and Theophil Wurm formed a Confessing Church that opposed anti-Semitism and the nazification of Protestant theology. In spite of Nazi efforts to silence them, they continued to oppose the Nazis throughout the war period, most of them becoming prisoners in Nazi concentration camps.

The Catholic church in Germany maintained stable relations with the Nazi regime into the war period. The Pope signed a concordat with the state in 1933, hoping to protect church freedoms. But as the state absorbed church property, restricted youth from access to religious instruction, and removed crucifixes from schools and hospitals, some Catholic officials voiced their concern publicly. But neither Protestants nor Catholics ever adopted an official condemnation of the Nazi racial policies. Protest against Nazi racial policies remained a matter of individual conscience; indeed, many church leaders were persecuted for publicly condemning Nazi anti-Semitism. Still, no concerted, broadly based religious resistance developed. And neither the Pope nor Catholic prelates entered official protests against the harsh treatment of Polish Catholic priests as the Germans took over their portion of that state.

Catholics and Protestants made their strongest anti-Nazi protests in 1940. The source of their alarm came from reports of a Nazi-sponsored euthanasia program launched to dispose of the mentally ill, the physically impaired, and mentally retarded persons. Opposition to these measures of the regime grew as the number of those receiving official notices of the "unexpected death" of family relations in government institutions increased and turned suspicion into certainty. Children reported seeing unfortunates shoved into vans (later dubbed "murder boxes") used for executions. In 1943 Bishop Clemens August Galen of Münster, delivered a message publicly exposing these actions. In the face of criticism, the regime suspended the program "for the duration." The Nazis, however, continued to perfect their gruesome techniques of mass killings, using them on Jews in the death camps in Poland.

THE INVASION OF RUSSIA

Hitler's ambitions for conquest and Lebensraum in the East were revealed when he began his invasion of the Soviet Union on June 22, 1941. Although German conservatives were relieved to end their partnership with the "Bolshevists," Hitler's action confronted the German people with the realization that the full-scale war they found themselves in was not likely to be of short duration. The pressure on the home front for stepped-up production of armaments increased. By the winter months of 1941, Hitler's first serious military misjudgments were underscored by the need for a public drive to collect winter clothing for the troops on the Russian front. At the same time thousands of Russian prisoners of war entered Germany. This new source of labor replaced the contributions of men who had departed for the front, but the Russians became a source of concern for domestic security. More anxiety came from English flights over German territory, which were meeting with less resistance because German planes and some antiaircraft pieces had been diverted to the Eastern front. The remaining 88 mm antiaircraft guns still brought down British aircraft with frequency, and the R.A.F.'s night bombing was not very effective. But the bombing reminded Germans that Britain remained unconquered.

During the heady days of 1941–42 Germans at home followed the progress of the armies as they marched ever deeper into Russian territory. Success followed success, and food supplies at home were bolstered by requisitioned grain supplies from the Ukraine. Still, shortages were noticeable, and "swap" advertisements appeared in the newspapers to help alleviate some civilian needs. As battles took their toll, the walls of more and more homes displayed the photographs of fallen soldiers embellished with the black *Hakenkreuz* and the circumstances of death. Soldiers on leave brought a "Führer package" of food to ease shortages at home. They also brought stories of the travail on the front and whispered of the cruel deeds of Nazi commissars operating behind the lines.

As though the stubborn opposition of Great Britain and the Soviet Union was not enough, only four days after the Japanese attack on Pearl Harbor Hitler added the United States to the official roll of German enemies. Perhaps Hitler's action simply formalized the long-running hostilities with America, but it obviated any internal debate among Americans about the need for war with Germany. In spite of the grievous damage inflicted by the Japanese, Roosevelt and the Allies made the defeat of Germany the foremost objective of the war. For those Germans who remembered World War I, Hitler's decision to provoke U.S. intervention was a fatal omen.

On the night of May 30–31, 1942, the first British thousand-bomber raid pelted the German city of Cologne. The planes deposited 1,500 tons of incendiary and explosive bombs on business and residential areas of the city. Four hundred seventy-four inhabitants were killed and five thousand were injured. By

World War II standards, the casualties were not huge, but whole sections of the city were laid waste. In all 45,000 inhabitants lost their homes. From this point on the German home front was in every sense of the word a battle front, and civilians found their lives drastically altered. For it was, indeed, the civilians who were the targets of the bombs. On February 22, 1942, British Air Marshal Sir Arthur Harris assumed the position of commander-in-chief of the British Bomber Command. Harris determined to carry out fully a new directive that sought to employ bombing attacks to destroy the morale of the German civilian population and of industrial workers in particular. Unable during night bombing to identify factories and destroy them, the British decided to kill those who worked in them. This was a harsh and cruel directive, but it had precedents: the German bombings of Warsaw and later of London and other British cities (certainly there had been little regard for civilians then). The Luftwaffe had also strafed civilian refugees in the conquest of France and most recently had conducted punishing raids over Soviet cities. Fighting for their survival and walled off from the Continent by Hitler's fortifications along the French coast, the British thought bombing would inflict the most punishment on the enemy. When the Americans joined in the air war against Germany, they, like the British in earlier days, still thought it possible to bomb during the daylight hours but raised no objections to the continued British night attacks. Like the British, they soon discovered that the German fighters could knock out sizeable numbers of the huge B-17 bombers dubbed "Flying Fortresses." Although the B-17s seemed formidable when they flew in close formations, they were armed only with machine guns. The faster German fighters often carried light cannon that could lob shells into the formations from a secure distance.

The Nazi regime labeled these raids as gangster and terrorist actions. It had, indeed, prepared quite well for such attacks. Most German cities had an adequate number of air raid shelters for their inhabitants. Antiaircraft defenses employed a million men. The warning system against attack was effective. Additional fire-fighting equipment had been supplied. After raids, relief services promptly provided clothing, food, hospital supplies, and damage payments. But continuing onslaughts and the demands of the Russian campaign gradually reduced the effectiveness of defense and relief efforts.

During the remainder of 1942 the British engaged in thirty-two more attacks on German cities. Approximately 12,600 tons of bombs fell on nineteen different targets, with Bremen being struck five times, Duisburg four times, and Essen, Hamburg, and Emden twice each. But this was only a modest beginning, and the hail of bombs would intensify markedly in 1943.

DOMESTIC SHORTAGES

The home front suffered from other problems besides air attacks. Food supplies dwindled steadily. To the normal civilian demands for food were added those of millions of foreign workers imported to labor in the munitions factories; commonly these laborers received rations only minimally above starvation levels. Fruits and vegetables (especially potatoes) were increasingly hard to find. Beer and wine were in short supply, even in the traditional areas of their production. Tobacco was scarce. The party encouraged resourceful souls to search for vegetables in nearby forests but German women showed little enthusiasm for what they regarded as a suggestion they should "graze" like cattle. Farmers felt they were being offered too low a price for their produce by the regime and resorted to increased participation in the black market, a practice which continued until Hitler's final days in spite of all efforts to control it.

Clothing shortages were also becoming severe. Early in 1943 clothing ration cards no longer allowed a person to buy new suits or coats, and people crowded the stores to see what they could get with their remaining rations. Other items of daily use were also hard to obtain. Only a tenth of those needing new shoes could get them. Cooking utensils and brooms were virtually unobtainable. Bed linen, toothbrushes and toothpaste, bicycle tires, and mattresses were scarce commodities.

Daily life also changed with the evacuation of many schools. Parents sent children away from areas susceptible to bombing attacks. Some mothers and children were also evacuated from endangered cities. In all over a million people had left urban areas by the end of 1942. Mothers worried over the welfare of children taken to strange and not always caring environments. Women evacuated to new homes had to share kitchens with their hosts, who often resented these intrusions into their privacy. Jealousy often flared between dwellers when one group seemed to have better rations or a better lifestyle than the other. All in all the atmosphere of life grew thin and stifling—the halcyon days of the earlier Nazi period had faded into dim memories. One began to concentrate solely on survival. The party still provided some public entertainment—gifted speakers presented readings of old and well-known poetry, and music, when one had the opportunity to enjoy it, was the best opiate against worry and fear.

BAD NEWS FROM THE BATTLE FRONTS

The grumpiness and sense of malaise which accompanied the domestic deterioration was aggravated by the growing concern for events on the Eastern front. Worry about the troops at Stalingrad increased as battle reports described the stalemate. Families who had been hoping for visits from soldiers in Russia due for furlough began to wonder whether their loved ones would survive the ferocious battles. News of Soviet attacks south of Stalingrad made apparent to the public the encirclement of German forces there. And, at the same time, Rommel's forces in North Africa began to reel under British attack. Anglo-American forces landed in North Africa on November 7–8, 1942.

Within Hitler's headquarters there was also great stress. Hitler kept expecting the ultimate capture of Stalingrad and turned away every suggestion of a strategic retreat. Göring promised that the Luftwaffe would supply the troops shut up in the *Kessel* (kettle) at Stalingrad, but the airborne provisions delivered were extremely scanty and occasionally utterly idiotic (one flight supplied contraceptives, food, spices, and propaganda pamphlets). In bitter cold, with short rations, confronted by fresh Soviet troops equipped with new T-34 tanks and massive artillery, the Nazi army at Stalingrad fought and died trying to realize their Führer's ambitions. On February 3, 1943, 91,000 survivors, including twenty-three generals and Field Marshal Friedrich Paulus, surrendered to the Russians. The last letters written by the soldiers in Stalingrad were never delivered; censors feared that the references to the horrendous fighting and the neglect of soldiers would weaken morale. But morale was weakened instead by silence. Hanging like a pall over the lives of thousands of families was the unanswered question of the fate of thousands of German prisoners of war in Soviet hands.

The tragedy of Stalingrad was closely followed by setback in North Africa, where the forces of the "Desert Fox," Field Marshal Erwin Rommel (who had left Africa after a decisive defeat at Mareth) surrendered on May 7, 1943. The British and Americans interred some 220,000 prisoners, but there was less concern at home for their survival than for those in Russian camps.

It was after the defeat at Stalingrad that Joseph Goebbels, speaking to a great crowd in the *Sportpalast* in Berlin on February 20, 1943, finally proclaimed total war. The aftermath of Goebbel's speech was accompanied by increased police action against real or suspected opponents. At this time too the Nazis pressed more German women to serve in the armaments factories. Until this time, Nazi ideologists had defined the proper role of women as that of housewives and mothers. Now there were larger efforts to enroll women in party paramilitary organizations and in factory production. But this development came too late, and the party's efforts to lure German women out of the home were not very successful.

FIRESTORMS IN HAMBURG

For those at home none of the catastrophes on the battle field rivaled the grim significance of the air raids on Hamburg, which began on July 24, 1943, and reached their peak intensity on the night of July 27. Other raids followed through the night of August 2. Hamburg had from the first been a prime target for British bombers. It was a port city. It was marked by waterways that made it vulnerable to night bombing. And it was Germany's second largest city. Hamburg was well prepared for air attack, possessing numerous shelters and abundant fire equipment, including 312 kilometers of fire hose. All of this preparation was put to the test by the first British raid on the night of July 24. A total of 740 planes left fires and destruction behind. But the fires were extinguished, communications restored, and morale remained relatively high.

The raid of July 27 altered this optimism. Climatic conditions assisted the work of the 712 bombers on this night, and Hamburg was engulfed in the first firestorm of the war. Cyclones of flame sped through many sections of the city, overtaking fleeing persons, draining the air from underground shelters, crumbling concrete structures, and destroying the fire equipment brought out to restrain them. Tales of the horrors on that night circulated throughout Germany, among them pathetic stories of children reduced to hardened skeletons and of mothers demented with grief carrying their remains about in suitcases. Not until the bombing of Dresden late in the war was such devastation repeated, but Munich, Cologne, Augsburg, Frankfurt, and Stuttgart all felt the wrath of the Allied bombers, some enduring minor firestorms as well. The cities of the Ruhr were repeatedly visited by destruction from the sky.

Just as the Germans had sought to increase the effects of their raids on England with the development of the V-1 and V-2 weapons, so also had the Allies added to their small incendiary stick bombs an arsenal of larger bombs filled with fluids that adhered to the structures they hit. Also unleashed were the huge "blockbuster" bombs designed to destroy whole sections of a city. Soldiers from the front who crouched in the cellars of target cities while these new weapons fell around them found the experience as shattering as their experience in battle. And the provision of disposable gasoline tanks allowed fighters and dive bombers ("Jabos"—hunter-bombers to the Germans) to reach eastern parts of German-held territory, where they sometimes chased people on the streets or menaced areas around the cities.

Meanwhile, the people experienced growing personal pressures—most of all shortages of food, leading to constant "hamstering" in the countryside to seek some morsel of food in return for old clothing, radios, or some carefully preserved family treasure. Factories demanded long hours of work, and more women sought employment in them. Old men and young boys were hastened to prepare fortifications against enemy intrusions and to serve in *Volkssturm* (people's militia) units. Boys of fourteen were taken from their families to "man" the antiaircraft batteries. Nazi leaders were increasingly vigilant against any kind of defeatism or critical comment.

The people studied their maps bitterly as places once the scene of brilliant victories marked the retreat of German forces across Soviet territory and into eastern Europe. And the hordes of foreign workers from the east, specifically Poles and Russians, were a source of worry for a home front so heavily depleted of its male population. In the buses Poles no longer got up willingly to give places to German women. Some workers sang the songs of partisans who harassed German troops on the Eastern front. And German refugees from the eastern areas began to arrive, their numbers growing as Soviet forces moved westward. Many of them told tales of wild flights made in wintry conditions without plans for safe transport; many also had no relative in Germany to receive them. With food short, clothing rations nonexistent, and many homes already filled with refugees from the bombing, these new guests on the home scene often met with a chilly reception.

THE FINAL SOLUTION

By 1942 Jews present on the home front had been transported by train to the death camps in occupied Poland. Most German citizens had at best a vague knowledge of their fate. Some loyal Nazis wrote to Goebbels suggesting that some of the millions of Jews in the hands of the German army be brought to the big cities as hostages against the continued air attacks. But many Germans suspected that Jews were not going to be a visible element in a victorious postwar Nazi Germany. The signs forbidding Jews and Poles from entering restaurants and other restricted places were often altered to remove the word "Jews" since they were no longer present. Some Germans showed small acts of kindness to Jews gathered for evacuation. In Berlin there were some sharp outcries against the deportations, and some prominent Catholic and Protestant churchmen registered protests against the treatment of the Jews. Those who held high church offices could get away with such defiance, but considerable numbers of lower level churchmen and churchwomen were punished severely.

The most serious organized protests against the Nazi policies came from a small group of students in Munich who founded the White Rose movement. Their main accomplishment was to distribute anti-Nazi publications called the White Rose Pamphlets. These tracts called upon their fellow students and the German people to rise against "the dictatorship of evil." The major conspirators, Hans and Sophie Scholl, their close friend Christopher Probst, and philosophy professor Kurt Haber, who had inspired them, were all guillotined. The wife of Professor Haber was left without support after the Nazis revoked his appointment. She even received a bill for wear and tear on the guillotine that had taken his life.

Perhaps in the presence of fanatical police measures nothing more could have been done to save the Jews. So determined were the Nazis to fulfill their "mission" that in the final stages of the war trains were used primarily to carry Jews to execution. Ironically, this task took priority over transporting refugees from threatened areas or even supplying reinforcements to areas in danger of Soviet attack.

HORRORS OF THE LAST DAYS

The last year of the war found the German people facing the cruel consequences of Hitler's war. Soviet forces moving across eastern Europe and eventually into Germany vented their rage on all who stood in their path. Hundreds of thousands of Germans streamed westward seeking escape from capture, rape, enforced servitude, and savage death. And on February 13 and 14, 1945, the city of Dresden was virtually destroyed by combined British and American air attacks. Although the original estimates indicated that as many as 135,000 persons lost their lives in the resulting fires, more sober estimates of 35,000 to 40,000 deaths have been calculated. But there was a cruelty in continuing raids on an already burning city, a deed that did not set the western Allies very much apart from the revenge-minded Soviet troops.

By April 1945 an ill and half-demented Hitler, ensconced below twenty-five feet of reinforced concrete in the bombed and beleaguered capital city, realized at last that he had played chess using forces which did not actually exist. In the end Hitler turned against the people who had given him their hearts and their hopes. Demanding death before he would yield to invading armies and the destruction of his country's cities, factories, and bridges, Hitler became the demigod who brought his world down around him because it had disappointed him. Here and there fanatical followers still died for the Führer. In other places those who had followed his wishes without question deserted their idol to greet the enemy as deliverers and seek their mercy. In the rubble of the cities those who had remained until the end were joined by people who voluntarily or involuntarily had left. They returned seeking remnants of broken homes and of friends and family members who had been scattered across the Reich. Thousands of refugees without food, clothing, or a means of existence also poured into the cities. Most remarkable was the staying power of the German people, who had seen the glory of victory give way to bleak defeat. They would endure some five years of occupation and the division of their country as a consequence of Hitler's war.

* * *

THE ITALIANS AT WAR

Mussolini was Hitler's ally during the first four years of the war. The German dictator many times credited Mussolini with having provided an example that he had followed. But to his countrymen Mussolini never quite achieved the godlike status of Hitler. It is true that he had suppressed all existing democratic institutions and had created a one-party state. But Italian Fascism never attained the ideological, semi-religious trappings of German Nazism. Mussolini himself did not seek to define Fascism until 1934, and even then portrayed it as a dogma of action, not a philosophical concept.

Most important of all, Fascism, unlike Nazism, never developed the machinery for the propagation of ideological concepts. The Duce had, indeed, created an aura of power that gained broad popular respect. To many Italians he stood for the defeat

of Communist dangers, the promise of dramatic domestic progress, and the establishment of international prestige. Mussolini
became a symbol of bravery, determination, and the will to act.
But his personification of these virtues did not extend to his major lieutenants, let alone to the semi-guerrilla leaders who had
followed his cause throughout Italy. Efforts of would-be propaganda experts such as Giovanni Gentile, Roberto Farinacci, and
Achille Starace fell far short of the accomplishments of Joseph
Goebbels.

Moreover, it is quite clear that Mussolini himself became increasingly unsure of himself and the direction of his regime as
the 1930s proceeded. He and his lieutenants had been in control
since 1922. They had created a kind of accommodation of interests between party, church, and business classes. Even some
workers and peasants came to support the regime. But the party
leaders and their programs were losing their vitality by the middle 1930s. Calls to heroism and toughness now replaced rosy
promises. Italian economic data began to reveal that the hoped-
for progress had not been realized and that Italian workers were
not better off than they had been before Mussolini. Even their
daily diet had not improved markedly. A sense of weariness and
querulousness pervaded Mussolini's relationships with his clos-
est associates.

Even during stable times Mussolini was constantly confronting the danger of internal opposition from his own *Fascisti*.
Throughout the 1920s and 1930s he undercut potential opponents
by "changing the guard," rotating his followers among the top
posts. He also had to keep an eye on two other rival authorities.
One was King Victor Emmanuel III, who remained titular head
of the state but who exercised no real power. The other was the
Catholic church, which Mussolini had won over by granting extensive concessions to its control over education and worship.
Liberal and left-wing opposition to the regime had always existed, but Mussolini remained reasonably well-accepted by the
Italian people until he brought them into World War II. Completely unprepared for this step morally or physically, the Italians were coupled with an ally that they never really liked or
trusted.

DECLINING POPULAR SUPPORT
FOR MUSSOLINI

Mussolini's earlier military ventures were relatively popular. The brief war over Ethiopia in 1935–36 achieved success quickly and stirred the imagination of the Italian people, who dreamed of a new Roman empire (although stories of Italian atrocities against their poorly armed and almost helpless enemies brought a considerable loss of sympathy for Mussolini in Great Britain and the United States). Italy also aided Francisco Franco in the Spanish Civil War on the grounds that Franco was upholding capitalism and Catholicism against godless Communists. The war provided some victories for Italian arms, but unsympathetic pro-Republican news reports and the rally of liberal and left-wing volunteers from Britain and the United States against the Spanish and Italian fascists again hurt Mussolini's reputation. Moreover, the human and financial costs of Italian aid were high and the war also provided experience in guerrilla warfare that would later be used by Mussolini's Italian opponents.

The rising military power of Germany confronted Mussolini with multiple dilemmas. Clearly he admired Hitler and the determination and will power which he exuded. He was flattered by the Führer's personal attention. In 1938 the Fascists, led by Achille Starace, the national secretary of the party, adopted anti-Semitic racial policies like those in Germany. An obscure professor, Nicola Pende, offered proof that there was an Italian race, a thesis he thought should be proclaimed as truth; Pende also claimed that the Hebrew race had no place in this racial order. His vague, absurd, and scientifically unproved theories were opposed by the Pope and the Catholic church. The anti-Semitic policies also drove many of Italy's best academics into exile.

Mussolini longed to share in the triumphs and territory that he hoped would come from an alliance with Germany. But Hitler was moving rapidly to war after his bloodless military move into the Rhineland and the unopposed *Anschluss* with Austria in 1938. At the Munich Conference Hitler let Mussolini assume a prominent role as Great Britain and France agreed to the partition of Czechoslovakia. Still, Mussolini was bitterly aware of his own nation's lack of preparedness and of his people's inherent dislike of military adventures. After Munich he hoped that Hitler would be content to pause before beginning a war. Mussolini's military leaders indicated that they needed three years to provide the equipment necessary to join a new war. The Duce, however, was desperately afraid that if he waited that long, the Germans would claim the territory and glory of a global empire, leaving Italy with virtually nothing.

Mussolini's diplomatic negotiations with Hitler on the eve of World War II met with alternating disdain and flattery. The German dictator continued to pursue his own goals on his own timetable, but now and again praised the Italian leader and cajoled him into feeling that his partnership was important. It was at this point that many Italians began to regard Mussolini as Hitler's Italian *Gauleiter*, a designation which became ever more caustic as Mussolini became more subservient to the Germans. For his part Hitler hoped that the Italian alliance might neutralize the British and French presence in the Mediterranean theater. As it turned out, Hitler's military actions would probably have been more successful if he had allowed Mussolini to remain neutral.

MILITARY BLUNDERS AND DEFEATS

As Hitler moved to war, Mussolini in April 1939 used the vestiges of military strength remaining from the Ethiopian and Spanish adventures to take over Albania. This conquest was not accomplished without problems since Italy at that point had only seventy-three divisions in its army, less than the country had had in 1914 at the beginning of World War I. It was the height of recklessness when Mussolini declared war against Great Britain and France on June 10, 1940. Just as foolishly, on August 4, 1940, he chose to invade British and French Somaliland, and a month later he sent troops into Egypt. On October 28, 1940, Italy attempted to invade Greece from Albania. Count Galeazzo Ciano, who as the war progressed became a critic of Mussolini and his pro-German policies, declared that Italy's armaments were in a "disastrous" state.

A long series of catastrophes followed. The Italian fleet suffered serious damage from British air and sea attacks. The Greeks repelled the Italian attack and moved into Albania. And weak British forces in Egypt began to roll back the Italian army and take thousands of prisoners. Before the Germans sent Erwin Rommel to back up the Italian actions in Africa in late February 1941, the British had captured 140,000 Italian prisoners. The course of events in Africa and in Greece began to change with German intervention, but Hitler's planned invasion of the Soviet Union had been delayed by the rescue action in Greece.

More Italian soldiers died or became prisoners of war in the months that followed. Mussolini sent 2,900 officers and 58,000 soldiers along with scarce trucks and planes to fight with the Germans in the invasion of the Soviet Union, and a year later he contributed ten more divisions, a total of 250,000 soldiers. Thousands of Italians were captured in Russia, and few of them returned from the cold and disease-ridden prisoner-of-war camps far north of their sunny homeland. Others died in the desert conflicts, where the skill and toughness of Rommel's Afrika Korps was not mirrored in the fighting of his Italian allies. Thousands of prisoners of war were added to those already in English camps (the British would hold more than 300,000 Italians at the end of the conflict). Little else could be expected when at least on one occasion fresh recruits, aged eighteen, were shipped overseas on the very day of their mobilization without even the most elementary training. That the Italian military leaders, his own Fascist followers, and the Italian people themselves so long accepted the criminally inept leadership of Mussolini seems incredible. It is clear that the Italians, unlike the Germans, really did not like war. Mussolini himself complained of their pacifism. Italians he remarked, were, "a race of sheep" who had to be beaten into heroic action. "To make a people great," he said on one occasion, "you have to send them into battle even if you have to kick them in the pants."

What did the Italian people think and feel in the midst of this situation? It is not easy to state simple answers. Italy's entry into the war had not been popular. Food and heat became scarcer as the Germans cut deliveries of wheat and oil. The Germans did not help to expand Italian war industries; they provided only the finished products and sought to boost their industrial production by enrolling many Italian workers. British and American bombing took heavy tolls on Italian cities—before the end of the war 10 percent of housing space, some two million rooms of civilian habitation, was destroyed.

Throughout the war the black market supplemented meager rations. The daily ration of bread was 100 grams—"a little black ball hardly filling your two hands," said one observer. The familiar *pasticceria* (Italian pastry) was completely forbidden. One could barter for food—the family refrigerator brought an acquisition of 100 kilos of flour, and a radio could procure 100 liters of cooking oil. If one got eggs, they had to be preserved in the bathtub with a lime mixture to keep them from spoiling. The government raised taxes and imposed forced loans. And the index of real wages continued to plummet throughout the war years. The regime muted its traditional emphasis on women's domestic responsibilities and recruited women for work in factories. In the midst of wartime shortages, many of these new factory workers were not able to take time to stand in the lines awaiting scarce goods, and home life eroded.

Thousands of Italian workers served in Germany. Even Mussolini complained about reports that they were shabbily treated. Until 1943 the Italians suffered and criticized but otherwise accepted their lot of a bad government and inept leadership. Mussolini himself was aware of defeatism within the party and the low morale in the country itself. The first industrial strikes since the establishment of party control took place in March 1943 in the Fiat factories in Turin. Sympathy strikes were staged in Milan. Women in significant numbers were among those shouting for peace and bread, overtime pay, and cost-of-living increases. And the first significant renewal of open antifascism followed.

THE FALL OF MUSSOLINI

Mussolini fell from power not because of popular opposition; he was ousted by the Fascist party itself. On July 24, 1943 (the meeting began on the afternoon of the 24th and the vote came early in the morning of the 25th!), the Grand Fascist Council, always previously a rubber stamp for Mussolini's policies, voted for his removal. King Victor Emmanuel III, who had been a vague symbol of royal authority during Mussolini's rule, accepted the decision of the council, named Pietro Badoglio as his successor, and acquiesced in Mussolini's arrest and imprisonment on the Gran Sasso, an elevated plateau in central Italy. Mussolini was, by this time, a mere shadow of his more dramatic earlier personality, his hair thin and gray, his face marked by age and weariness.

Many Italians reacted to his removal with joyous demonstrations. A newspaper commentator noted that three years of war had underscored the inanity and impotence of Fascism that had brought Italy to the verge of disaster. But the country's trials were not over. The Italians would have a long wait before they were able to take control of their own destiny.

Great Britain and the United States had already invaded Sicily by this time. They greeted news of Mussolini's fall with pleasure. They were wary, however, of the new government led by Badoglio, who had commanded the Italian forces in the Ethiopian campaign. As events were to prove, the Allies were too eager to force an Italian surrender before the new government could secure firm control over the country. When that surrender took place on September 6, 1943, Germany occupied the country with troops and security forces and initiated oppressive action against those who opposed their control. The two subsequent years of fighting up the Italian peninsula were arduous and costly as German troops offered desperate resistance, aided by the country's harsh topography.

Mussolini, after his defeat in the Grand Fascist Council, remained a prisoner on the Gran Sasso, where he lived in a hotel accessible only by elevator from below. Hitler freed Mussolini from his aerie-like prison in a dramatic rescue. The SS officer Otto Skorzeny engineered the escape on September 12, 1943. Hitler had still retained his admiration for the Italian leader and brought him to Germany, where he received Mussolini courteously and made provision for his return to Italy. The Duce's status there, however, clearly was that of a puppet of the German government. Theoretically Mussolini was in control of the northern part of Italy, where he proceeded to establish a new regime, but his authority was dependent upon German support. The Germans pressured him to take vengeance on his monarchist and Fascist opponents, particularly the anti-Nazi Count Galeazzo Ciano. And after a strange trial in which five major conspirators were condemned to death (although they professed continued loyalty to Mussolini), the sentence was carried out in a typically bungled execution; the work of the firing squad had to be finished off with the pistols of those supervising the event.

THE NEO-FASCIST REGIME

Mussolini, supported by Hitler's forces, set up a new regime in northern Italy, one professing a "republican" and more socialist character than the earlier Fascist state. Mussolini was happy with this return to his earlier socialist roots (which he embraced prior to 1921) but distressed by his dependence on German support and by the fact that Germany had placed *Gauleiters* in control of Italy's northern provinces, which contained a combination of German- and Italian-speaking inhabitants. His republic was named after the town of Salò, where the major governmental offices were established, but Mussolini spent most of his remaining days in Gargagno near Lake Garda. All of Italy south of this area, including the city of Rome, was under German control and direction, although Fascist militia in these areas continued to cooperate with the German forces.

Mussolini's days under Nazi tutelage were spent almost as if he were in retirement. His dalliance with his latest mistress, Clara Petacci, was discovered by his wife Rachele, who was outraged by this liaison. Mussolini rather quickly became convinced that the war was lost and kept importuning Hitler to make peace with the Soviet Union. On only one occasion did Mussolini show his independence from the Germans, making a public speech on December 16, 1944, in Milan. Even at that late date, he could still elicit applause from partisan crowds. To the end Mussolini had a certain appeal to many Italians.

Most Italian military forces had been interned in Germany. And more Italian workers became poverty-stricken "guests" in Germany, their woeful condition attracting pity even from hardened observers. Symbolic of Italy's decline were the thousands of paper Italian flags stored in the German propaganda ministry that were consigned to the scrap heap.

For the first time Italian guerrilla action against Fascists and Germans gained broad support. Committees of National Liberation brought together a wide array of political affiliates ranging from the Communists to moderate Catholic groups. Former Fascist troops discarded their uniforms and weapons, which were appropriated by those who fought the Germans. Very shortly after the fall of Mussolini a popular uprising in Naples succeeded in turning out the Germans before the Americans came into the city. In northern Italy, both before and after the return of Mussolini, the Communists, who had never ceased hating the Duce, joined forces with many other disaffected groups. The Groups for Patriotic Action found thousands of new recruits ready to accept the dangerous life of making and using bombs and explosives against German and Fascist installations. Women contributed significantly. The Women's Defense Groups, founded in Milan in November 1943, came under the loose supervision of the proliferating Committees for National Liberation. Victoria de Grazia estimates that 70,000 women were enrolled in the Italian resistance before the end of the war. Women were frequently employed as *staffetas* or couriers, relaying messages or handling administrative duties. They communicated orders from unofficial resistance headquarters, had lists of contacts and "safe" houses, and distributed pamphlets and weapons. A woman feigning pregnancy could conceal explosives under her clothes, and a market basket filled with apples could disguise a load of hand grenades earmarked for fellow conspirators. De Grazia states that 4,600 women were arrested, tortured, and tried, and 2,750 were deported to German concentration camps. Another 623 were executed or killed in battle.

Particularly in the northern part of the country, guerrilla groups demonstrated that Italians could fight effectively when the objectives were ones they really believed in. The numbers of these guerrilla forces grew during the last two years of the war. Some scholars have estimated numbers of above 100,000, but no conclusive figure has been set forth. In Italy, as in France, there were instances of brutal reprisals for guerrilla actions that took the lives of German soldiers. One such slaughter occurred in the town of Civitalla della Chiana on June 18, 1944. Eleven days later SS troops of the Hermann Göring Division were guided to the town by a local Fascist militia and machine-gunned 250 men.

As in France also, Italian resistance fighters suffered torture and death when they fell into the hands of the Germans. In Rome itself the Nazi torture chambers were particularly brutal in their treatment of real or suspected opposition leaders. And there, as in other parts of Italy, many Fascist leaders attached to Mussolini's old order continued to abet the Germans in every way possible. Nevertheless, thousands of Allied soldiers, Jews, and Italian resistance fighters seeking escape from Nazi persecution, found considerable refuge offered by Catholic clergy. Controversy remains, however, concerning the actions of Pope Pius XII. Would it have been advantageous for him to have publicly denounced the Nazi anti-Semitism (with the possibility of arousing retributive action by Italy or Germany), or did he best serve the resistance by encouraging this undercover, haphazard kind of assistance? The question has been much debated during the postwar period. Undoubtedly in the later stages of the war, when desperation governed Nazi policies, Germany would have exacted punishment for a papal *pronunciamento*. At any rate, Italy was one of the very few points of egress from Europe for Jews who had somehow escaped from France or Germany. Considerable numbers of them secured refuge in the Vatican and in other church installations in the city of Rome. Largely due to the actions of the Catholic church, 80 percent of Italian Jews survived the war.

THE ALLIED CAMPAIGN IN ITALY

Meanwhile, the British-American campaign into Sicily had begun on July 10, 1943. Italian troops offered token resistance, but German forces fought well and, as they left Sicily for the mainland, preserved most of their manpower, equipment, and munitions. Negotiations for Italian surrender had begun shortly after Mussolini's fall, but debate over the terms of an armistice (the Allies took pains to make it appear to be an unconditional surrender) went on until suitable statements were signed on September 3, 1943. With this act the Italians ceased to be allies of the Germans, but neither were they accepted as allies against the Germans. The premature announcement of the surrender on September 8 allowed the Germans to occupy Rome and fortify areas to the south of the capital. The scene was set for a difficult and protracted campaign up the forbidding terrain of the peninsula.

Italian sympathy was clearly on the side of the British and American forces through the remainder of the fighting. But the occupying Germans, now freed from the pretense that the Italians were allies, tended to drain away all remaining domestic resources. And the oppression in the territories that they occupied increased in severity. The most egregious example occurred in Rome in response to a partisan action on March 23, 1944, in which a forty-pound bomb exploded on the Via Rasella, taking the lives of thirty-three German SS soldiers. (Most of them were older men, newly enrolled for this service in Rome, and had been recruited from northern Italy rather than Germany proper.) German officials scurried around, emptying prisons of those already condemned to death and adding innocent victims to obtain the 330 persons (ten for every German killed) required for the retaliatory execution. Those slain were taken to one of the Ardeatine caves outside of Rome, later to be marked as a shrine for those executed.

The Allies were very cautious about dealing with the Badoglio government. American political advisers preferred abolishing the monarchy and at the very least thought that not only Victor Emmanuel III but also his son Humbert should have been passed over in the succession to the throne. They tended to yield to the British on this matter since the latter regarded Italy as a part of its Mediterranean sphere of influence that it expected to control in the postwar period. Moreover, both the British and the Americans were concerned with the strength of the Communists in the Italian resistance movement and were unwilling to see Italy join the growing group of states under Soviet influence. American and British forces set up occupation regimes as they moved northward and made efforts to "purify" (*epuration*) conquered territory, but mafia and camorra leaders, somewhat restricted under Mussolini, tended to reclaim their familiar positions of power. Neither the British nor the American military found very competent personnel to assume the administration of occupied areas in the early period of the fighting. It was very easy for some appointees to abuse their positions of authority for personal advantage, and this problem would continue to plague the Allies into the postwar period.

Some of the most difficult fighting of World War II took place in the Italian campaign. The hardships of the troops moving north against the Germans at Cassino and at Anzio were more severe even than those faced in the Normandy invasions. In Italy the Allies confronted cold, damp, muddy terrain and suffered very heavy losses inflicted by crack German troops entrenched in almost impregnable positions and armed with withering firepower. Anglo-American forces in the Italian campaign enlisted a Polish unit and divisions from New Zealand, India, Canada, France, Algiers, and Morocco. Cemeteries are testimonies to the cost of the campaign. A thousand Poles were buried near the monastery at Monte Cassino, which they had taken at the sacrifice of most of their forces. In another cemetery at Cassino 4,266 British subjects were buried. A French cemetery at Venafro contains 3,414 graves. At Nettuno 7,812 American dead were buried. Another British cemetery contains 3,369 graves.

The campaign north to Rome was long and tortuous. The Allies entered the city on June 4, 1944 (the Americans had, somewhat reluctantly, been accorded the honor of being first). They were heartily welcomed by the Italians, for the liberated people needed relief measures. Rome's population had been left in the most extreme straits, for the retreating Germans had seized food and materiel as they left. The Allies accomplished minor miracles as they restored order. One day after the Allies occupied Rome the little black bread ball was replaced by honest-to-goodness white loaves.

But larger miracles came with more difficulty. The Committees of National Liberation had ostensibly sought to coordinate political groups ranging from Christian Democrats on the right to the Communists on the left. Yet the strength of the Communists in the guerrilla ranks had made them a dominant element in the resistance movement. Shortly after the Allies occupied Rome, the government of Marshal Badoglio was replaced by a new six-party government under Ivanoe Bonomi; it was a government lacking any real authority. As the Allies pushed north, the Communist strength in these regions was evident by the increased support for Palmiro Togliatti, who had earlier returned to Italy from Moscow. But British and American political advisers, aware of the Soviet infiltration in Poland, Czechoslovakia, and the Balkans, were not willing to support a Communist regime in Italy. Allied military administration, as it was established, tended to tolerate the return of mafia and camorra leadership in the south and to support conservative leaders in the north.

Disagreement continued between British and American representatives on the Allied Control Commission. A vexing question was the establishment of the exchange rate for the Italian lira. The advantageous exchange rate enjoyed by American soldiers during the early phase of occupation allowed many of them to become wealthy racketeers during their stay in Italy. On the other hand a stabilization of the exchange rate might have allowed Italy an unwarranted advantage over the British and other European states in international trade. As it was, the drain of purchases of scarce commodities partially due to these determinations initiated a rapid rise of inflation, and the lira began the precipitate fall which troubled the entire postwar period.

As the Allies moved northward from Rome, the occupation authorities encountered additional evidence of Communist strength in the partisan groups. Florence chose a city government controlled by Communists. And in other places Communists spearheaded antifascist activities. Probably too little credit has been given to the contribution Italians made to the liberation of their country in part because the movement was so heavily dominated by the Communists. Some 232,000 Italians took part in the partisan movement and 70,000 died in the period from 1943 to 1945. In addition, 50,000 Italian troops took part in the last battles along the so-called Gothic Line, and the Italian navy aided in the last portion of the fighting while the Italian airforce aided in supplying the resistance groups in Yugoslavia.

It was the Communists who delivered the *coup de grâce* to Mussolini. The former dictator with his mistress, Clara Petacci, had been fleeing to the north, aided by loyal supporters. On April 28, 1945, he and Petacci were captured and executed by partisans. Their bodies were later exhibited, hung face down from a girder on a filling station in the little town of Dongo where fifteen Italian hostages had been executed during the previous August. Not until more than ten years later was the grave where he was buried decorated with the fasces.

Mussolini left behind no real legacy for his former supporters to carry on, although neo-fascist candidates in some elections would invoke his memory. His granddaughter has become a political figure in her own right. But in periods of difficulty and unrest some Italians have not shaken the feeling that times were more secure during the 1920s than they have been since the end of the war.

Indeed, the early postwar period was one which saw continued hardship and travail for the Italians. The country's industrial complex had been neglected during the war years. Supplies of needed food and clothing were to be desperately short for some time after 1944. Only the fear of Communist takeovers spurred the United States and Great Britain to ameliorate Italy's economic problems. But the unsettled political situation contributed to a chaotic postwar period. In the north the strength of the Communists revitalized and radicalized the labor unions in that industrial region, while the continued backwardness of the agrarian southern area, the *Mezzogiorno*, was to be for many years one of Italy's most serious economic problems. Fascism was eliminated, but the Christian Democrats continued to battle the Communists on all fronts; the Communists likewise refused to join in coalitions with their Catholic opponents. As a consequence postwar politics in Italy were as chaotic as they had been before the takeover by Mussolini.

Perhaps one might conclude that the German civilians, who had been more successfully mobilized for war than the Italians, learned more from defeat. In Germany it became a kind of aphorism that political participation was required to prevent the return of such a leader as Hitler. But Italians, who had suffered much under Mussolini, could only look back on him after his fall as a buffoon who had been manipulated by Hitler. Through myriad cabinet coalitions the Italian people lived much as before. Politics remained, as it always had been, secondary to the loyalties of family, church, and local customs.

5 / POLAND AND
THE HOLOCAUST

No book dealing with the trials of civilians during World War II can pass over the monstrous tragedy inflicted on the Jews of Europe. More than 5.8 million Jews lost their lives. They were cruelly seized from their homes, herded into cattle cars for long railroad trips without food and water, and driven into sadistically run concentration camps where, deprived of all hope and dignity, they were stripped naked and packed into hideously conceived execution chambers.

It was not that Jews had not known persecution in earlier centuries. They had been expelled from Spain in the sixteenth century. In tsarist Russia they had suffered in pogroms. There and in other countries of eastern Europe they had lived in ghettos. And there was the terrible example of the Dreyfus case in France, where an innocent Jew had almost lost his life serving a prison sentence at Devil's Island.

But the twentieth century had seemed more secure. Jews had attained visibility in French politics. In Germany they had not only owned banks but published newspapers. They were prominent across Europe in music, art, and the learned professions. Social barriers still existed and anti-Semitism continued, but most prejudice was largely attributed to extremist groups. Before Hitler's rise, Jews felt more secure in Europe than they had in many past centuries.

Hitler's coming to power in 1933 was accompanied by anti-Semitic propaganda and persecution. Storm troopers raided Jewish stores and beat up Jews on the street. Jewish lawyers and officials lost their status and rights. Fines, beatings, and pogroms gave warning of what was to come. Strangely, however, the number of German Jews murdered in the Final Solution was less than in many other parts of Europe. More than half of them had been able to emigrate before the outbreak of war, although the Nazis later gathered up some of them as they occupied other countries in western Europe.

THE DESTRUCTION OF POLAND

Poland, the first victim of German military aggression, was to lose the largest percentage of its Jewish population in the Final Solution. It had, indeed, had the largest Jewish population of any country of Europe. Of the 3.3 million Jews living in Poland before World War II, 3 million of them died in German extermination camps. Poland was chosen as the site of the death camps not because the Nazis regarded the country as sympathetic to such an action, but because the Nazis regarded Poles also as subhumans fit only for extermination.

Poland had fought alone in the first campaign of the war. The British and the French were professed allies, but they were unable to provide any real assistance. A French attack into German territory might have helped. The Siegfried Line, across from the French Maginot Line, was not as strong in the fall and winter of 1939 as it seemed. But both allies were committed to defensive strategy. German planes strafed and bombed Polish cities, towns, villages. German armies routed the outmoded Polish armed forces, and 200,000 Polish soldiers were killed and wounded, with 420,000 taken prisoner. As the Germans established occupation, Nazi administrators burned 531 towns and villages and executed 15,376 Poles. But the Poles had done a little better in the fighting than was commonly believed—the Germans lost 45,000 men, 697 airplanes, and 993 tanks. These losses and the heavy expenditure of ammunition, added to the later losses in the campaign in France, left the Germans short of men and equipment needed for the invasion of the Soviet Union two years later.

At the same time that Germany swept through the western part of Poland, the Soviet Union occupied the eastern part that it had demanded in the secret protocol of the Soviet-Nazi Non-Aggression Pact. This zone, approximately 46 percent of the area of Poland, was quickly overrun by Soviet troops. Because this region contained a mixed population, Lithuanians and Ukrainians as well as Poles, the Russians claimed that the inhabitants of the annexed territory had welcomed the police action and had voted to be incorporated into the Soviet Union. Some of those who voted for annexation were mobilized into the Soviet army.

The Germans divided the western portion of Poland into three parts. An area in northwest Poland was formed into *Reichsgau* Danzig-Westpreussen. The city of Danzig had remained principally German during the interwar years, and the Poles had countered this fact by building the port of Gdynia to secure a separate outlet to the Baltic. Obviously Danzig would lose its significance in the new arrangement, hence the pro-German element had been critical of the Poles. South of this zone the Germans created a second "German" state, *Reichsgau* Wartheland. The cities of Łódź and Poznań were to be Germanized (de-Polandized) and renamed, respectively, Litzmannstadt and Posen. Upper Silesia became a part of the German province of Silesia.

The rump portion of Poland, after the Soviet excision of territory on the east and the German annexation on the west, was labeled the General Government of Poland. It was placed under the supervision of a German administrator, Hans Frank.* Although supposedly remaining separate from the German Reich, it was by no means independent. The Germans intended to use both it and the newly created *Reichsgau* Wartheland as a resettlement region for German colonists. Some of these prospective settlers would come from the Reich itself, but many would also come from ethnic Germans transferred to Germany from the Soviet Union during the period of cooperation from 1939 to 1941; some Germans also came from the Baltic states of Estonia and Latvia, absorbed by the Soviets in 1939, others from Soviet-occupied Poland, Bessarabia, and Bukovina. Estimates of Germans resettled in Poland or Germany proper range from 650,000 to 750,000. There had also been an expectation that Polish land might be made available to farmers from Germany itself—from Baden, the Rhineland, Württemberg, Franken, and the Sudetenland.

---

*In one of those strange vagaries common to the Third Reich, Hans Frank, in speeches in the summer of 1942, denounced the police state and the arbitrary action of the police and the SS in Germany. He was stripped of his party offices but allowed to remain as Governor-General of Poland until called to the trial at Nuremberg.

Obviously the welfare of the Poles was not going to interfere with the prosperity of arriving German citizens. From the very first the Germans regarded the Poles as subhuman and therefore deserving only extermination or enslavement. As the Jews of Poland were pushed into ghettos in most Polish cities, the Poles themselves were subjected to harsh German treatment. Poland was to become a labor pool for the master race.

Theory became practice as the shortage of workers in agriculture and industry within Germany claimed the attention of Nazi administrators preparing for military action in the West. Subsequently occupation authorities enlisted Poles to work in Germany, luring some with "contracts" that seemed to promise treatment comparable to German workers. But very quickly pretenses of legality and of voluntary compliance disappeared. Contrary to the Geneva Convention's rules for the treatment of prisoners of war, 344,000 Polish POWs were used in Germany's 1939–40 agricultural harvest. The trains later used to convey western European Jews to extermination camps were employed in this period to convey Polish workers west to aid on the farms and in the factories. Nearly 800,000 civilian workers, about a fifth of them women, had been brought from Poland to Germany by the spring of 1940.

But the requests for more workers seemed never to end. Frank was notified in January 1940 that another million male and female workers would be needed, including 750,000 agricultural workers, at least 50 percent of whom were to be women. By late autumn 1943, 1,123,000 Polish males (29,000 of them POWs) and 527,000 women were working in the German Reich. For this large number of Poles, their wartime home front was spent far away from home in a country among people who hated them (and whom they hated). Dressed in deteriorated clothing marked with the Polish "badge" (a violet "P" on a yellow triangle), they could not make use of public transport unless required for work. German clergy provided some church services, but there was no social or cultural entertainment. Germans were warned against aiding Poles, and severe penalties were imposed for sexual improprieties. As the war went on, food dwindled, clothes fell apart, decent shoes were unobtainable, sickness increased, and the death totals rose.

Some Poles received better treatment. In one of the most ghastly acts of the Nazi period, thousands of Polish children who were blonde and blue-eyed and showed other traits befitting the Aryan race were taken from their parents and shipped to the Reich, where they were trained in Nazi youth homes to become members of the master race. Nazis examined other older Poles for remnants of German ancestry and racial characteristics and gave them the opportunity to be "Germanized." Since the choice was either participation or probable execution, many Poles embraced the obvious alternative.

For the most part, however, the Germans exercised wholesale cruelty toward the Poles. They liquidated the greater part of the Polish intelligentsia, closed Polish schools and universities, executed a considerable percentage of the country's Catholic clergy, and destroyed remnants of Polish art, architecture, and cultural treasures. By war's end Poland had lost 45 percent of its physicians and dentists, 59 percent of its attorneys, 15 percent of its schoolteachers, 40 percent of its professors and many of its journalists.

GOVERNMENTS IN EXILE

As these events took place, the Poles were without capable representation abroad. President Ignacy Mościcki and other members of the Polish government had been interned in Rumania. Many members of this government had been followers of the late Polish Marshal Josef Pilsudski, who had seized control of the government in 1926. In attempting to establish its legitimacy in exile, the deposed government found itself discredited by the defeat of the Polish army and its clearly failed management of foreign policy. Moreover, it was linked with some anti-Semitic policies and actions in the prewar period.

Mościcki exercised his prerogative of choosing a successor as president, naming Wladyslaw Raczkiewicz, who was regarded as less of a Pilsudski-ite than most members of the previous government. But he found a government in exile already forming under General Wladyslaw Sikorski, who had assumed control of the remnants of the Polish army that had escaped to France; Sikorski named himself premier. Although Raczkiewicz tried to name an alternate premier, he did not succeed, and Sikorski retained his position until killed in an air crash on July 4, 1943.

Established first in France and then moved to Great Britain, the Sikorski government from first to last had opposition both from Great Britain and from Polish groups, especially those military leaders who had been in Pilsudski's entourage. Sikorski sought to create a government that clearly represented a majority of Polish opinion. But he could not and did not want to have a government which could not rally support within Poland.

The British hosts of this government in exile were disturbed by the dissension among the Poles. Morever, representatives of Jewish agencies declared that it was anti-Semitic. An additional complication developed when Britain became an ally of the Soviet Union after the German invasion in June 1941. Soviet aspirations in eastern Europe clashed with the strong position of the Polish government, which wanted to recover its prewar boundaries. British diplomats were predisposed to side with the Soviets and accept the boundary consequences of the Nazi-Soviet pact, particularly because that boundary coincided closely with the Curzon Line, drawn at the end of World War I.

Sikorski established the Union for Armed Struggle as the major agency for internal opposition to the Germans in December 1939. The Union divided Poland into six regions, each with its own commander. Sikorski named General Kazimierz Sosnkowski as head of the Union in London and General Stefan Grot-Rowecki as commander in Poland. But other resistance groups were also formed in Poland, and real unity was never achieved. Underground newspapers were published and sabotage actions carried out, but General Tadeusz Bór-Komorowski, who succeeded Grot-Rowecki upon the latter's arrest and execution in 1943, still classified the Polish resistance as "a conglomeration of commanders and detachments, whose attitude to one another are [sic] frequently undisguisedly hostile."

Perhaps this was unavoidable. Travel in occupied Poland was difficult, conspiratorial meetings always dangerous, rivalries and suspicions hard to overcome, and efforts to coordinate anti-German actions in different regions of the country almost futile. That anything was achieved is remarkable. Providing arms and ammunition was much more difficult to accomplish in Poland than in occupied France, since air drops from Britain were virtually impossible. Polish resisters did manage considerable sabotage of the railroads. Underground statistics claimed that 6,930 locomotives were damaged and 4,300 military vehicles damaged or destroyed, a total of 25,000 acts of sabotage. The Germans also had to replace a sizeable number of defective military parts because of Polish underground activity. These and other actions against German administration brought harsh retaliation. But the Poles' greatest contribution to final victory over Germany was their delivery to Great Britain of the Enigma coder for German military messages, a contribution which provided major assistance in deciphering the secret communications of the German forces; the intelligence gathered warned the British of the German V-2 rocket experiments at Peenemunde and enabled them to recover and deliver to Britain a defective V-2 rocket.

THE FINAL SOLUTION IN POLAND

Meanwhile, as has been seen, the Nazis had determined to make the Polish General Government a colony for German repatriates from the Baltic states and Soviet territory. Here, too, the Nazis established concentration camps at Auschwitz-Birkenau, Majdanek, Treblinka, Chelmno, Sobibor, Belzec, and Gross Rosen. These installations were the first death camps, since most of the prisoners died, but not until late 1941 did they function primarily as the execution camps for the Jews. At first the Germans had moved Jews into ghettoes in all large Polish cities, where starvation and sickness took a heavy toll. The real beginning of the Final Solution came with the German campaign in the Soviet Union. There the *Einsatzgruppen* of the SS carried out mass murders of the Jewish population with a savagery and cruelty which staggers the imagination. Victims were forced to strip and stand helpless while the execution squads shot them down; the bodies fell into great trenches dug for rapid burial. Death squads used sealed vans to asphyxiate Jews for the first time in Russia. The vehicles were first used in Poland in December 1941 at Chelmno north of Łódź. Early in 1942 Heinrich Himmler sent to Poland Christian Wirth, who created static death chambers into which were piped exhaust gases from diesel engines. Belzec was opened on March 17, 1942, with six gas chambers capable of murdering 15,000 people a day. Sobibor followed in April with an "output" of 20,000 human beings a day. Treblinka, northeast of Warsaw was equipped with 30 gas chambers capable of executing 25,000 daily. And Maidanek followed.

Auschwitz was the first extermination camp to use the prussic acid gas, Zyklon B, originally sold to kill vermin. Zyklon B proved the most effective method for the rapid killing of humans. Satisfied by the results, Himmler ordered on July 10, 1942, the liquidation of the entire Jewish population of the General Government, to be completed by the end of that year. Savagery and sadism accompanied the prisoners who entered these camps and were disposed of quickly and efficiently. Guards responsible for the executions often appropriated the money, jewels, and other valuables that these unfortunates brought with them. Polish Jews were, of course, joined in the gas chambers by those from the Soviet Union, from eastern Europe, and from western Europe, until the total of those killed approached six million. Certainly the term "Holocaust" is aptly used to describe this kind of destruction of life without limits, without pity, without regret.

The contributions Poles themselves made to the destruction of the Jews remains debatable. Poles sheltered some Jews; the estimates run from 40,000 to 120,000. Whether these victims received adequate shelter is also a matter of controversy. Considering the degree of cruelty that German troops displayed, and the certainty that they would severely punish any kindness shown to Jews, even these figures are remarkable. It is known too that the Polish secret army supplied some arms to the Jews in the Warsaw ghetto uprising, January 18–22, 1943. Obviously they did not provide enough to be effective—ghetto fighting continued until May 8 but few Jews survived. In fact the Poles themselves did not have the arms to take on German tanks and heavy weapons. More Poles helped Jews avoid the death camps than the minority who informed on them. Moreover Poles were not enrolled as guards in the death camps. (That role was assigned to selected Ukrainians and Lithuanians.) There had been and remained some incidents of Polish anti-Semitism, but these acts did not receive any official support from the Polish government in exile or from resistance groups sponsored by it.

That Jewish historians and those Jews politically active at the time of the Holocaust should feel outrage at the apparent lack of concern for the enormous killing taking place is understandable. Less understandable is the attitude of world leaders who learned details of the Nazi genocide. One can only suggest that they may well have considered the reports which came to them as exaggerated. Certainly American public opinion did not fully react to the reports of atrocities until military units overran some of the concentration camps within Germany itself. Then, too, anti-Semitism among some influential government members in Britain may account for the tardy response. This suspicion derives in part from Britain's unwillingness to open Palestine to Jewish refugees, but in the midst of a war of great extent and difficulty, the British government could not afford to outrage Arab feelings by flooding that state with a tidal wave of Jewish immigrants. A feeling of helplessness may also explain the lukewarm response to the Holocaust. Ever since the war, the question has been raised as to why the death camps were not bombed. This question, however, assumes a kind of precision bombing in which execution chambers and railroad lines would be destroyed but the prisoners left unharmed. This capability was beyond the technology of Allied bombers. Even with the use of fighter-bombers that carried the throw-away gasoline tanks to increase their range, it would have been necessary for western pilots to find landing places in the Soviet Union once the mission was completed. And the fate of the air drops intended to aid the Warsaw uprising indicates that accuracy from the air often left much to be desired. But, in retrospect, one could wish that some attempt had been made. Even with failure, even with the potential death of as many inmates as of guards, one could still say, "We tried."

The Poles themselves continued to suffer until the end of the war. The significance of their own resistance activities remains debatable. But resistance against the German military was never very effective unless the resisters had some safe havens where men could be trained, organized, and armed. This was never available to the Poles. Some fought effectively in the army of Wladyslaw Anders formed in the Soviet Union, but the Soviets never trusted them and did not give them a real opportunity to fight the Germans. Hence the Poles usually perpetrated isolated acts of sabotage and reprisal, many of them quite effective.

As the war progressed, Polish relationships with the Soviet Union worsened. The Soviets claimed that most of the area they had incorporated in 1939 had been in effect assigned to them by Lord Curzon, the British representative who had attempted to settle that boundary line at the end of World War I. Having integrated this area into the Soviet Union proper, it was clear that they had no intention of returning it to Poland after the war.

In April 1943, a Berlin radio broadcast reported the discovery of the bodies of some 3,000 Polish officers who had been shot and buried in the Katyn forest. The Germans blamed these slayings on the Russians, and Polish authorities were prone to agree. (An American congressional investigation after World War II confirmed this judgment with documentation that seems to stand even after the end of the Cold War.) This incident, along with reports that Poles in the Russian occupation zone had had no voice in the plebiscites by which that territory was annexed to the Soviet Union, strained further already bad relations. Under British pressure Sikorski had signed with reluctance a treaty of cooperation with the Soviet Union on July 27, 1941, although the proposed eastern boundary for Poland had not been set. But partisan movements in the east were heavily dominated by Polish Communists and never fully cooperated with Sikorski's resistance movement. Within that eastern zone the Communists branded Sikorski's followers as fascists and created their own Polish Committee of National Liberation.

THE WARSAW UPRISING

The shape of Poland's postwar trauma was adumbrated in the events surrounding the Warsaw uprising. Russian forces had advanced to the eastern side of the Vistula River and were reasonably close to the Polish capital. Russian radio broadcasts called for the people of Warsaw to rise to assist in their liberation. At the same time a considerable number of German citizens and armed forces were fleeing westward. Although the Polish under-

ground had not had a favorable experience in its efforts to cooperate with the Soviets, it was also anxious to establish a stake in
Poland's postwar government by being the first to free its capital
city. General Tadeusz Bór-Kamorowski called for the rising on
August 1, 1944. Much damage was inflicted on the Germans, but
the fighting of the resistance groups was not well organized or
directed. The Poles failed to seize the bridges across the Vistula,
the nearby airfields, or any strategic points necessary for lengthy
resistance. The German forces in and around the city were
stronger than had been anticipated, as the Russians were also to
claim at a later time.

Nevertheless, the German forces, although aware of the rumors of insurrection, had not been well prepared. Hitler ordered
the destruction of Warsaw in reprisal and ordered General Erich
von dem Bach-Zelewski of the Waffen SS to quash the uprising.
This turned out to be more difficult than the Germans had anticipated. Meeting resistance, the SS forces of General Mieczyslaw
Kaminski, a refugee from Soviet labor camps, and of General
Oskar Dirlewanger, a sadistic leader in his own right, engaged in
the most brutal repression of Warsaw's citizens. The Germans
executed women and children as well as men; plunder and rape
accompanied these actions. Some of the worst atrocities were
halted when Bach-Zelewski restored some modicum of discipline after August 5, but he moved methodically to clear away
the Polish resistance groups. German units had weakened resistance forces by uncovering large stores of their weapons before
the uprising and had also discovered that the resisters were hiding in the sewers and so stopped off the passages. The final fighting in the old section of Warsaw lasted from August 19 to September 2. In other areas of the city fighting continued through
the end of September. Offers by the British and Americans to
drop weapons and supplies to the insurgents were turned back
by the Russians, who would not let western planes land on Soviet airfields. Soviet air drops were insufficient and poorly chosen. Anglo-American air forces did finally deliver some supplies
on September 18 and went ahead to land on Soviet fields. The
Polish forces finally surrendered on October 2, 1944.

The German forces took severe measures against the resistance in the days which followed. There seems to be some truth

to the Russian claim that the Warsaw rising was launched prematurely—apparently the radio broadcast which set it off had not been sponsored by the Soviet military. Nearly 300,000 Poles lost their lives in the fighting. When the Russians finally entered the city in January 1945, they found nine-tenths of it utterly destroyed.

By this time, the Soviets had already established the Lublin Committee to direct the future of postwar Poland. This Communist-dominated group became an obvious rival of the Polish government in exile in London. Negotiations followed between Stanislaw Mikolajczyk, a representative of the prewar Polish Peasant Party, and the Lublin Committee, but agreement proved difficult. Arguments about the future of Poland and the fate of the members of the western-sponsored Polish resistance groups arrested by Soviet authorities marked the first events of the Cold War. A "western" leader, Mikolajczyk, was added to the Lublin Committee, but it was clear that Poland, after being dominated by the Germans for six years, was simply acquiring a new master.

The thousands of Polish laborers in Germany were returned to a state where the Jewish population had been virtually wiped out. Russian-sponsored Communists put them to work in collective farms on which they were not much happier than they had been in Germany. Church leaders returned also, and the Polish masses rediscovered the long-deprived solace of religion. But the Poles had to wait over forty years before they became the real masters in their own homeland. Of all the nations of Europe, Poland's history during the war was the one most washed with the blood and tears of martyrs, both Christians and Jews.

The enormous losses to modern civilization resulting from the Nazi occupation and Holocaust is often too much for the mind to grasp. One can only imagine the great literary masterpieces, the marvelous musical creations, the profound treatises in the fields of philosophy and religion, and the advances in science that never were because of the genocide that took place on the soil of Poland. And the fact that such heinous crimes could happen left both Christians and Jews shaken in their belief in God's direction of the universe. Perhaps a new century will provide new roots for faith in reason and progress.

6 / OTHER HOME FRONTS

By 1942 the military forces of Germany had conquered at least temporarily a vast stretch of territory from the northern reaches of Norway all the way to the Mediterranean on the south, and from the Atlantic coast of France eastward to the Soviet Union. This conquest was accompanied by occupying armies and military administration. The role and responsibility of this purely military administration was never clarified, and myriad party and governmental groups feuded over the disposition of new territories. It is obvious that Heinrich Himmler anticipated that this vast block of territory would be under his administrative control, whether absorbed into a greatly expanded Reich or made into vassal states meant to serve the desires and ambitions of an Aryan central Europe. But other Nazi leaders and agencies wanted to run conquered nations to suit personal ambitions. This situation, as well as geography and the racial stock of the subject peoples concerned, affected the conditions of occupation. As a consequence there were great variations in administrative arrangements.

PRESUMED ARYAN STATES: THE LOW COUNTRIES AND SCANDINAVIA

Belgium and the Netherlands were the first two western states conquered by Germany. King Leopold III remained in Brussels but refused to exercise power while Belgium remained under military occupation. A government in exile in London continued to regard Belgium as being at war with Germany. But the Belgian government had from the first anticipated defeat and German occupation. The finances and business controls of the state were highly centralized in the Société Générale, the oldest and most significant of the Belgian banks. The Société Générale had financed the state's ventures in mining and industry and achieved

great success during the nineteenth century. In the period between the two world wars, it extended its control over every major section of industry. Other Belgian banks became intertwined
with it. The list of businesses it financed was lengthy—coal mining, iron and steel, zinc smelting, shipping, sugar refining, and
tobacco processing among them. It also had significant holdings
in Congo mines and plantations.

In World War I Belgium had defended itself against Germany
and, while occupied, heroically resisted cooperation. But this
stance had cost a substantial loss of materiel and forced hardships on its people. During their occupation the Germans had
also sponsored separatist groups who worked to detach the
Flemish portion of the state. As a consequence, Belgium in the
post–World War I period divided into Wallonia, where French
was the official language, and Flanders, where Flemish was the
official language, with Brussels left as a bilingual area. Leopold
III sought to escape a repetition of the sad consequences of
World War I by a policy of neutrality, but he also sought to prepare for Belgium's defeat and occupation by Germany.

Belgium's industrial strength and reputation had faded in the
aftermath of World War I. Much of its industry, especially that
of iron and steel manufactures, industrial chemicals, railroad
equipment, and textiles, was not only very much outmoded but
also resistant to modernization. Even talk of reform, which
would have required some infringements of individual economic
freedoms, carried with it opposition to political and economic
liberalism.

In World War II, Belgium fought against Germany for four
days. On the fifth day, May 28, 1940, Leopold III surrendered un-
conditionally. The Belgian army had lost 12,000 wounded and
8,000 killed. Millions of refugees had fled the country. The cabinet had also departed but was willing to come back after surrender. The Germans, however, refused permission. Leopold and the
Belgian bankers, meeting together in a consortium, agreed to
collaborate even before the German occupation began. Leopold's
efforts to win support from the victors got little sympathy. At a
personal meeting with Hitler on November 19, 1940, he advanced
three wishes—1. a recognition of the independence of Belgium;
2. the release of Belgian prisoners of war; 3. an improvement

of the Belgian food situation. Hitler sent him home without any concessions.

The Germans assigned command in Belgium and northern France to General Alexander von Falkenhausen, counted as one of the more humane Nazi administrators of occupied territory (he had had earlier connections with military opposition to Hitler, but he displayed no disloyalty during the occupation period). Eggert Reeder, who had been a German regional administrator in Cologne, saw to the administration. In Reeder's complex arrangements many Belgian administrators continued their activity, although some were replaced with figures from the Flemish fascist movement. But German business groups were also encouraged to take a role in bringing Belgium into the German system of production.

Much plundering occurred during the early days of Nazi occupation. Solders shipped home trainloads of items in short supply. Factory stocks were confiscated. Nevertheless major German industries established ties with their Belgian counterparts—steel, coal, and textile works most significantly. Banking ties between Belgium and Germany also developed. Belgian bankers agreed without protest to transfer to German authorities heavy occupation payments and to devalue the Belgian franc, which severely reduced the wages of Belgian laborers but also allowed some domestic production to continue. The most damaging action of the German occupation was inflicted by a campaign launched by Reich Marshal Hermann Göring in 1942. In an effort to dry up the Belgian black market, Göring determined to buy up any and all kinds of black market products at whatever prices might be asked. The result was soaring inflation, and almost everything of value was drained off to Germany. The suffering of Belgian workers greatly increased, and a number of them accepted labor assignments in Germany.

Pro-Nazi groups such as the Rexists were strong in Belgium, especially in Flanders. During World War I Germany had tried to incorporate Belgium into its empire, and some old-timers were happy to see the return of German troops. A considerable number of Belgian young people took part in Nazi-sponsored athletic and social events, and the country's major pro-Nazi leader, Léon Degrelle, became an SS *Sturmbannführer* and was decorated with the Oak Leaves Order. Although he later made disparaging comments about his membership in the SS, Degrelle's unit fought with the Nazis until the bitter end. Other Belgians were also recruited for military service on the Eastern front.

Belgium had been a home to some 90,000 Jews prior to the German invasion, with the largest number living in Antwerp and Brussels, the remainder in smaller cities. Some of these were refugees from elsewhere—Germany and Poland most prominently. Anti-Semitic policies were quickly established, including exclusion of Jews from most businesses, restrictions on the education of their children, and the establishment of required dwelling areas within the cities. Jewish councils, controlled by the Germans, administered these areas. Deportations to Auschwitz began in 1942 and continued well into 1944; many others died from hunger, disease, and overwork before being sent to the concentration camps. Many Jews were hidden by Belgians and escaped death. Some 20,000 survived the maelstrom of the Holocaust.

The Belgians themselves also suffered. Almost a quarter of a million Belgian men and some 30,000 women were working in Germany by the end of the war. Nazi depredations placed everything in short supply, and hungry people walked about in shoes that scarcely served to keep out the rain and snow.

As in France, the resistance movement in Belgium was always the work of a small minority, but it was an important one, since it participated frequently in the rescue of British and American airmen who came down in enemy territory. The resistance plotted escape routes through France to Marseilles and even across Spain to Gibraltar. It was a Belgian nurse's aide named Andrée de Jongh, whose code name was "Dédée," who established the Comet route which was responsible for the rescue of one thousand airmen, escaped prisoners of war, and other endangered persons. Dédée was arrested in 1943 and sent to Ravensbrück concentration camp but survived the war.

The Netherlands had an even stronger Nazi movement than Belgium. Andreas Mussert, the Dutch Nazi leader, organized mass demonstrations that looked almost as impressive as those staged in the early days of the Third Reich. Before and during the war he recruited some 110,000 followers, and Dutch representation in the Waffen SS exceeded that of other western European states.

The government of the Netherlands was in the firm hands of Arthur Seyss-Inquart, who had presided over the *Anschluss* with Austria. He had no intention of sharing controls with local leaders. Already many national figures had fled to safe haven abroad. Queen Wilhemina had escaped to London to lead a government in exile. From there she continued a strong line of resistance to the Germans which was to win for the House of Orange a much better wartime legacy than the monarchy in Belgium. Despite this opposition, Seyss-Inquart was able to use the local civil service to run the country and encountered little difficulty during most of the occupation. When a general strike broke out on February 25, 1941, the German army brutally repressed it and martial law was imposed. Over a quarter of a million Dutch workers were employed in Germany during the war.

The strength of the native Nazi movement made it difficult for those Dutch who were inclined to save Jews from the death camps. Some 140,000 Jews had lived in Holland before the war, 30,000 of them refugees from Germany and Austria. The usual routine of registration, confiscation of property, establishment of forced labor camps, and isolation within the cities was carried out. Some Jews were hidden by sympathetic Dutch citizens—the most famous case was that recorded in *The Diary of Anne Frank*. (A similarly impressive story of the efforts of the Dutch resistance to save some of Holland's Jews is Leesha Rose's book, *The Tulips Are Red*.) Some children were blended into Dutch families and thus escaped death. But with strongly anti-Semitic neighbors all around, sheltering Jews was more dangerous than in other western countries. Seventy-five percent of Dutch Jews perished in the Holocaust.

Like other countries under Nazi control, the Germans controlled food supplies for their own purposes. A Dutch resistance movement provided aid to Allied pilots and information to the British military. Its real strength was not fully felt until the closing days of the war. After Allied troops moved into Belgium and liberated the first Dutch city, Maastricht, on September 13, 1944, there was great rejoicing throughout Holland. The red, white, and blue flag of Holland was accompanied by a sea of orange emblems worn by the people of the city to honor the royal family. Free Holland radio called on September 17 for a general railroad strike to aid the Allies in the anticipated liberation of the country. But the campaign stalled, failing to take the city of Arnhem and a key bridge across the Rhine River. Allied military strategists redirected the campaign through Belgium and into Germany, leaving the northern portion of Holland still in German hands.

Seyss-Inquart had warned against the strike (only 1,500–2,000 of the 30,000 Dutch railway workers had failed to heed the call), and in retaliation the Germans closed off all inland shipping and confiscated bicycles, cars, and stocks of wholesalers. This left the Dutch with rapidly dwindling supplies of food that had to be procured on foot or on bicycle trips to the countryside. The winter of 1944–45 found stocks of food gone, electricity and fuel supplies unavailable. In the cold and darkness of this winter many Dutch perished. The Dutch premier of the government in exile, Pieter S. Gerbrandy, sought aid from the Swedes, who were willing to provide it, but Churchill and the Allies feared it would simply be confiscated by the Germans. The Germans had, indeed, destroyed harbor facilities in Amsterdam and Rotterdam as well as in other smaller cities. Parts of Holland became flooded as the pumps that kept out the sea waters failed because no electricity was available to run them. Swedish ships finally were permitted to dock on February 13, 1945. There was still some difficulty keeping the supplies away from the Germans, but Swedish help solved most of these problems. Yet, food shortages continued on into the spring. Not until April 29, 1945, were arrangements cleared for a massive food drop ("Operation Manna") into still-occupied Holland.

Seyss-Inquart remained in Holland until the news of Hitler's suicide was broadcast on May 1. German forces in Holland finally surrendered on May 4, 1945. By the time the Allied forces occupied the country it was estimated that at least 5 percent of the population of this northern area had reached a stage of extreme starvation. Nearly 18,000 Dutch men, women, and children had died of hunger in this final period of the war. These were added to the death toll of 104,000 Dutch Jews, 23,000 of whom died in air raids; 5,000 of whom died in concentration camps, and 30,000 of whom died in forced labor in Germany. The cost of the railroad strike of 1944 had been high, but it had restored Dutch pride and allowed the country to return to the massive task of reconstruction.

After Poland, Norway had been the second victim of Nazi aggression. The German invasion on April 9, 1940, had come in response to an anticipated British effort to establish holdings at Narvik and Trondheim. British forces put up a brief and spirited resistance, as did the Norwegian military. But the German troops had moved rapidly to occupy the capital, Oslo, and other principal cities as well as the airports and coastal fortifications. (The Norwegians did manage to sink the German heavy cruiser *Blücher*.) The south of Norway capitulated early, and with the withdrawal of the British from Narvik on June 7, King Haakon VII and his government boarded the British cruiser *Devonshire* to begin his exile. Haakon notified his people that further resistance was useless.

Norway was in German eyes considered an Aryan state. The Nazis tended to accept the "Nordic character" of Norway, Denmark, and Sweden as qualifying them for Aryan nationhood. Some Germans, with government sponsorship, made a scientific study of Norwegian records for the purpose of documenting their Aryan background. This basic racial concept had been featured in the writings of Vidkun Quisling, who had been the leader of a local movement called the *Nasjonal Samling* (National Assembly), a group that claimed a heart-and-soul affinity with German National Socialism. His movement had gained a respectable following in the prewar era among Norwegians, although it was not strong enough by itself to dominate the government, educational institutions, or labor and business organizations. But it was strong enough to encourage Hitler to believe that the German invasion would receive willing support in Norway. Quisling's name became synonymous with shameful collaboration and treason.

The military occupation of Norway, of course, was occasioned not by Germany's desire to protect an indigenous Nazi movement, but by the urgent necessity of preventing the British from securing the Norwegian coast and interfering with the shipping of Swedish iron ore to Germany. (Sea routes from Sweden were frozen during most of the winter, and so the ore was shipped across Norway and then brought by sea to Germany.) The resulting military occupation of Norway, as elsewhere in Europe, was brutal and efficient. Quisling assumed control but quickly proved unable to form a government which had any broad support. Hitler soon directed that Quisling be given an honorary post until he and his party could be educated in the task of leadership. Although Hitler continued to think that Norwegian Nazism could be strengthened, Quisling's party remained an insignificant one throughout the German occupation.

Hitler named a German civilian, Josef Terboven, who had been the *Gauleiter* of Essen, to be the *Reichskommissar* for occupied Norway. Terboven recruited most of his administration from Germany rather than from Norway. In exercising those powers, he often confronted the excessive demands of the German army, commanded in Norway by General Nikolaus von Falkenhorst. In the end, Norway was administered not as a partner but as a defeated enemy. The press was censored, the police placed under the SS, and regional Nazi authorities were established.

The Norwegian state the Nazis occupied was not a healthy one. Although territorially it was a third larger than the United Kingdom, Norway had a population of only three million. It could not feed itself or the animals on its farms. Only 3 percent of the land could be tilled and only a fourth was forested. Most of its territory was a mountain wilderness. The only cities with populations over 100,000 were Oslo and Bergen. Before the war Norway had to import most of its food and raw materials and depended upon its shipping industry for survival. From the first, therefore, Norway's precarious economy presented the Germans with a serious problem.

The military proceeded to improve the airports and fortify the harbors and coastline against potential invasion. The total strength of the occupying forces ran between 300,000 and 400,000; thus building barracks and providing food for these unwanted guests taxed Norway's strained resources. This problem worsened as the Germans sought to improve the country's infrastructure for military purposes. They added to the railroad system, improved shipyards, and built new power stations. But the Norwegian economy could in no way support this kind of financial burden. German-appointed civil authorities attempted to hold the line on these expenditures but had little success.

To add to Norway's already considerable exploitation, German economic planners attempted to bring Norway into line with German war production. Schemes were drawn up to expand Norway's aluminum production and to increase the country's output of artificial silk and cellulose, iron ore from the north of the country, high grade fertilizer, pyrites for artificial rubber and artificial textiles, and copper ore. Most of these schemes, which never went beyond the planning stages, were drawn up as Germany began to face the threats of invasion from both east and west. The economic union of the greater Reich became stillborn, but Germany's down payment on these big plans left Norway with a staggering internal debt.

There was an active resistance. A secret military organization came into existence, but surrounded by a ruthless occupying army that made it nearly impossible to import arms, it had to act with discretion and care. Here as elsewhere under German control, precipitate action usually triggered severe reprisals. Underground groups circulated newspapers and made plans for a rising when outside assistance became available. Almost 43,000 members belonged to the pro-Nazi *Nasjonal Samling* in 1942, making Norway a difficult place to organize and conceal resistance groups. Communist agents, particularly influential after the Soviet armies began to move westward, contributed also to the resistance, but their presence made Western observers uneasy.

Norwegian military officers who escaped to Britain were trained by British intelligence agents and engaged in daring coups. Although the actions of the British S.O.E. (Special Operations Executive) were probably not as dramatic or successful as some accounts suggest, they did demonstrate to the Norwegian resistance that their country had not been forgotten. Still, British undercover activities and raids on coastal areas occasioned severe reprisals against villages where they occurred; Nazi authorities burned houses, killed cattle, sank the fishing vessels, and deported male inhabitants to Germany. The most famous of the coups planned by S.O.E. took place on the night of February 27–28, 1943. It was directed against the heavy water operations at

Norsk Hydro in Vemork, and the destruction it wrought on this installation hampered the production of material used in German atomic energy experiments. A year later, on February 20, 1944, a joint Anglo-Norwegian operation sank a ferryboat loaded with the accumulated supply of heavy water. These daring feats provided a major contribution to final victory.

Norway was freed by the surrender of Germany in May 1945. The country's internal resistance had been defiant and proud to some Norwegians, but to others it had been too weak and too cautious to merit accolades for its accomplishments. In the aftermath of the war, Norway, like most liberated areas, tried those suspected of collaboration with the Germans. Vidkun Quisling, after a long and somewhat bizarre trial (it included a strange encephalographic examination to determine his sanity), was executed by a firing squad on October 24, 1945.

The Danes wrote an unusual chapter in the story of occupied states. King Christian X and his government remained despite the Nazi occupation and continued to exercise authority until 1943. Supposedly Denmark remained independent and neutral. The king had asked for his people to display "an absolute correct and dignified behavior" and continued himself to ride on horseback through the streets of Copenhagen, greeting the Danes he met on the way but ignoring the salutes of German soldiers. At the same time the Germans sent General Leonhard Kaupisch to keep peace, and he pledged respect for the freedom of the Danish people. For three years the Danes lived a relatively normal existence and were left alone for the most part by the German occupiers. The press, however, was controlled by a Danish quisling, Erik Scavenius, who headed the Foreign Ministry and worked for "mutual active cooperation" with the Germans. There was a Danish National Socialist Workers Party, but its popular support was minimal.

Schools and churches continued to operate normally. The Danish Jews were not disturbed. The Danes ate well and also exported food to the Germans. Some new Danish torpedo boats were turned over to the German navy, and about one thousand Danes were sent to the Russian front in 1941, where they suffered heavy casualties. Resistance groups were not very active in this period—the Danes were living too well to consider sabotage.

In 1942 things began to change. The king celebrated his 72nd birthday on September 26, 1942, and returned a rather curt "thank you" to a note of congratulations from Hitler. The German dictator in response sent a tougher army officer, Lt. Gen. Hermann Hanneken, accompanied by a German plenipotentiary, Dr. Werner Best, who was told to "rule with an iron hand." Scavenius was to head an acceptable new cabinet. But Best became quite sympathetic to the Danes and reported, probably fairly accurately, that they were "sick and tired of the war" and not likely to engage in sabotage. He pointed out that his civilian staff was miniscule in comparison with that of the much less populous Norway and emphasized that the Germans needed to preserve the goodwill of Danish farmers, who were making a significant contribution to the German food supply.

In early 1943 the apparent harmony began to erode. The British began to bomb the shipyards in Copenhagen, for some of the installations there were making diesel engines for Nazi submarines. The Danes also became aware of the increasing difficulties of the Germans in the Soviet Union, and British S.O.E. agents began demanding more support from the Danes. Sabotage increased, and in August 1943 a strike movement spread across the country. Shipyard workers in Odense precipitated the action, and sympathy strikes followed elsewhere. The Germans reacted by demanding a million *kroner* payment from the city of Odense and a complete capitulation of all anti-German action elsewhere. On August 29, 1943, the Germans imposed a state of emergency. The Danish army "surrendered under protest," and the Danish navy sank its own ships to prevent their seizure.

It was in the aftermath of this protest that the Germans planned to strike against the Danish Jews. Both Best and Hanneken were opposed to the action, but Himmler sent his own agent and police forces to carry it out. A Nazi official, George Duckwitz, played an unusual role in this story by warning Danish friends of the planned roundup of Jews. What followed was the most dramatic event in any occupied country—the wholesale hiding and saving of nearly all the Jewish inhabitants of the country. Some 8,000 men, women, and children were smuggled to Sweden on Danish fishing boats. Although most Danes acted on humanitarian grounds, some demanded considerable

amounts of money from the Jews as the price for their cooperation. A very few Jews, who had somehow missed the warnings of
friends and neighbors, were captured by the Germans.

Increasing sabotage of German installations in Denmark continued in 1944. The Allied invasion of France was accompanied
by strikes and violence in Denmark, and martial law was imposed. Troops also cut off water, gas, and electricity in Copenhagen. The Germans brought up cannon, arrested Danish police,
and sent several thousand Copenhageners to Germany. Allied
Mosquito bombers raided Gestapo headquarters in Copenhagen
in October 1944 and repeated raids in March 1945. Toward the end
of German occupation participation in the black market swelled
and the crime rate increased.

German forces in Denmark surrendered on May 4, 1945, and
the British arrived several days later. Montgomery gained the
plaudits of the people of Copenhagen when he visited on May 12,
1945. By that time acts of revenge against collaborators had begun, and scores of women were accused of having been too
friendly with the Germans. But Denmark was one of the few
countries on the Continent that still had surpluses of food at the
end of the war and can probably be counted as the occupied
country that suffered least from the German occupation.

THE FATE OF CZECHOSLOVAKIA

Czechoslovakia was the first fruits of Nazi aggression, conquered without arms but nevertheless a conquered state. Left
without allies at the Munich Conference in 1938, it had ceded to
Germany its "alien fringe" of the three million Germans in the
Sudetenland. Six months later, under Nazi pressure, it was
forced to recognize the division of the state into its Czech and
Slovak components; the Czech portion became a Nazi satellite
and was renamed the Protectorate of Bohemia and Moravia.

The two dominant nationalities in Czechoslovakia had dis-
agreed frequently during the interwar period. Bohemia had
been one of the prominent sites in the birth of Protestantism
during the Reformation, although twentieth-century Czechs
were not as devoutly religious as their sixteenth-century ances-
tors. The Slovaks were Roman Catholic and for the most part

peasants; they were more attached to the church than their western neighbors. The interwar leader of Slovak Catholics, Father Andrej Hlinka, died on August 16, 1938, and was succeeded by Monsignor Jozef Tiso who, along with other Slovak leaders, had been pressured by the Germans to demand autonomy. Prior to 1938, Hlinka and his followers had not sponsored this demand. The Slovak quisling, Vojtech (Béla) Tuka, along with Tiso and other members of the Hlinka party, enlisted the help of the Germans to make Slovakia a separate, authoritarian state. Tiso claimed that the Slovaks were "an individual nation, different from all others in their blood, language, spirit, culture, and peculiarity of country." Tied to these considerations was the strength of the Catholic Church, so dominant that one author called Slovakia, "the Parish Republic."

The Hlinka Guard became a Nazi-like supervisor of the social and economic life of Slovakia after its separation from Czechoslovakia. Slovakia also imprisoned units of the Czech army, many of which became partisan guerrillas or later joined the Red Army. Some 100,000 Slovaks were employed in Germany, but their earnings were not transferred home—the Germans simply noted that they owed a debt for these payments. This "debt" had reached a level of two billion crowns by 1942. Meanwhile, the families of these workers had to be supported by the Slovak state. Here, as in France, the Germans set an exchange rate for Slovak currency that was grossly unfair, allowing them to buy what they wanted cheaply but forcing the Slovaks into an inflation that made all their daily needs more and more expensive.

The wartime history of the Slovak state was not a happy one. There were some personal gains for Slovaks from the seizure of Czech and Jewish property. Some Slovaks found employment with the new government, and Nazi influence led to some material and status improvements for Slovak peasants and workers. But intraparty rivalries continued, and the state remained dependent upon Nazi support.

Partisan resistance to German control and the Tiso government existed largely in the mountain areas in the east. Many of the partisans were Communists, and the movement of Soviet armies westward added to their strength. Like the Poles, the

Czechs and Slovaks were to learn that the Soviet armies were not the liberators they had promised to be. A national uprising on August 24, 1944, heavily influenced by the Slovak Communist Party, resulted in Tiso's request for German troops on August 30, 1944. The SS squelched the uprising, punished those involved or supposedly involved, and deported Slovakian soldiers. Later in the fall, as Soviet troops advanced into Slovakia, the leaders of the Tiso government fled the country. Tiso, hiding in a monastery in Austria, surrendered to the U.S. Army and was later tried for his wartime actions.

The Czechs bore an even larger brunt of German mistreatment than did Slovakia. As the army moved into Prague in March 1939, Nazi economic experts took over the banks and the industry of a prosperous state. Worthless paper credits were offered in return. Thirty million dollars in gold was taken to Germany. As in Slovakia, the exchange rate between the Czech crown and the German mark favored the Germans. In addition the Germans charged an annual "war contribution" for the "protection" their armies offered the Czechs.

Edvard Beneš, the president of the Czechoslovak state, had resigned after the Munich Conference. His place was taken by Emíl Hácha, who found himself confronted by new complaints from the Germans. The Germans pressured the Slovaks to request German intervention, and troops also moved into the Czech area and created a new entity called "the Protectorate of Bohemia and Moravia." Although Hácha on a radio address used the term "reunification" of the Czechs and Germans, this new entity was neither completely a part of the German state nor completely independent.

Konstantin von Neurath was the first administrator of the Protectorate, overseeing the harsh economic measures and the arrest of Czech Jews. Hácha continued to act as State President. A new premier, General Alois Eliáš, was appointed—Neurath was to refer to him as a "prudent man." In this early period the Germans displayed some restraint. Hácha enjoyed a position similar to that of Pétain in France. He set up a National Solidarity Movement and appointed a National Committee to replace the parliament. Many Czechs hoped that reasonable conditions of occupation would remain. There was some justification for this feeling. The Germans were anxious to preserve a high level of armament production and foreign trade to obtain needed foreign exchange. They actually raised wages for many workers to cut down on trade union opposition, and rationing in the first years of occupation was more generous than in Germany itself. And Czech workers, unlike so many others in German-occupied territory, remained employed at home rather than being sent into Germany proper.

The price Czechs paid for their favorable treatment was the extension of more German controls and the presence of more German officials. Some factory managers and foremen were named publicly as potential hostages to prevent sabotage. More German police arrived—Karl Hermann Frank, the leader of the SS stationed in the Protectorate, was not happy with the relatively mild treatment of the Czechs under Neurath. In the fall of 1939 he found the occasion for punitive action.

October 28, 1939, was designated by resistance groups as National Independence Day. Czechs were to wear their best clothes, display the national tricolor, but not to challenge the Germans. The crowds grew during the course of the afternoon. Students were joined by workers. There were shouts favoring Beneš and Stalin. A police crackdown followed and Jan Opletal, a student, was killed. On November 15 Opletal's funeral was attended by 3,000 Czech students singing patriotic songs. The Czech police dispersed them. But this did not satisfy Frank. German police paraded; Czech students were arrested and sent to concentration camps; nine more students died before a firing squad.

This event was followed by the application of German racial policies in the Protectorate. German became the official language in schools and universities (most of the latter were closed and scientific equipment appropriated). Marriage and citizenship legislation was adopted. Some Nazi anthropologists had found the Czech "race" reasonably acceptable—unlike most eastern Europeans, they had fair hair and elongated skulls. But mixed marriages still had to be approved, with applications including at first nude photographs of prospective partners.

Hácha continued to cooperate with the Germans. Beneš, in exile in London, opposed concessions to German demands. But considering the geographical position of Czechoslovakia, and the rapid conquest of Poland, France, Belgium, Norway, and Denmark, Beneš's call for internal opposition to Nazi controls, heroic as it sounded, was not practical in the existing circumstances. Beneš broke with the Hácha government when it welcomed the German invasion of the Soviet Union. But some increase of resistance activity in the Protectorate did lead Hitler (as Frank had wanted from the first) to replace Neurath. It was not Frank, however, but Reinhard Heydrich, the chief of the German Security Police, who assumed office.

Heydrich's arrival was accompanied by police repression. Before his arrival the Germans had debated whether the Czechs should be assimilated or eliminated; Heydrich clearly stood for the latter, wanting to crush Czech resistance through terrorism. Almost 6,000 Czechs were arrested and 414 executed, including generals, professors, and officials. Among those arrested was Prime Minister Eliáš, who "confessed" to plotting treason and was executed. Anti-Jewish action resulted in 102,000 arrests in 1942 alone. Theresienstadt, a fortress town, was established as a transit camp on the way to the eastern death camps. Every element of business, the press, and cultural life became subject to the state.

In the midst of these events Hácha had threatened to resign but was persuaded to retain his post. He addressed the people, asking for complete submission to the Germans. Heydrich selected a new cabinet for Hácha headed by Emmanuel Moravec, the leader of a Czech fascist group called Viajka ("the Banner"). No Czech opposition was raised against the deportation of Jews—only 424 of the 94,000 Czech Jews were hidden from the Germans.

In London, the S.O.E. sought to increase Czech resistance. On December 28, 1941, two agents, Jozef Gabčík and Jan Kubiš, parachuted into the Protectorate. They remained in hiding for five months before they had the opportunity to bomb the car of Heydrich in the suburbs of Prague on the morning of May 27, 1942. Although Heydrich was not killed outright, he died several days later. Frank took the opportunity to show his leadership. Martial law was proclaimed. Frank proceeded on Himmler's orders that 10,000 Czechs were to be arrested at once and shot 100 of them that same day. Kurt Daluege, the chief of Germany's regular police, was named as Heydrich's successor. Frank offered a reward for the arrest of Heydrich's murderers that reached twenty million crowns, but not until June 18 were the two men found in the Orthodox Church of St. Cyril and Methodius in Prague. They committed suicide before being taken.

Six hundred Czechs were shot in the two weeks following. On June 10 the reprisals reached a new level of horror with the total destruction of the Czech town of Lidiče, accompanied by the execution of its entire male population. On June 26 the village of Lezaky received a similar punishment except that the women were killed as well. But the Germans never fully broke the spirit of the Czechs, who after 1943 saw more reason to believe that their travail would eventually end.

Edvard Beneš had remained the head of the Czechoslovak government in exile throughout the war years. He had repeatedly visited Moscow and Washington while working with the British leaders. His cabinet included Slovaks as well as Czechs. As the war drew to a close, however, it became clear that Beneš's government was in jeopardy, since Czechoslovakia, like Poland, was going to fall within the sphere of Soviet influence. Late in 1944 and into early 1945 the Soviets pushed the Germans out of Slovakia and entered Bratislava on April 4, 1945.

By this time American forces under General George Patton had reached the western frontier of Czechoslovakia. They could have taken Prague before Soviet forces arrived there, but political agreements between the western Allies and the Soviet Union had reserved that privilege for the Russians. Czech citizens revolted against the Germans on May 5 and took over the city. But the German forces in the Protectorate did not heed the unconditional surrender agreement signed by the German High Command on May 7, and a number of Prague's citizens died on the 8th before the Germans gave up the fight and Soviet forces reached the city. Beneš returned as the leader of a coalition government committed to economic reform but not to complete communization. But the sad truth was that one occupying force had once again been replaced with another. Over forty years would elapse before Czechoslovakia really became free.

FIRE IN THE BALKANS

As noted above, civilian resistance was found everywhere in conquered German territory. Sometimes it was silent, reflected in mute hostility and grudging acceptance of a situation that could not be altered without rescue from abroad. On other occasions, brave but often futile acts of violence and sabotage lashed out at enemy forces. But really significant guerrilla warfare against the Germans was confined largely to the Soviet Union and the Balkan countries. The story of the partisans in the Soviet Union has been told in an earlier chapter, although many nuances and details of their deeds and accomplishments still await a fuller accounting. The history of the partisan movements in Yugoslavia and Greece has received greater attention, although the narratives are often filled with conflicting details and judgments. Partisan movements in the Balkans achieved greater success than elsewhere in Europe. In the rugged hills and forests of an historical region of dark ethnic and religious rivalries, the Germans confronted the only native partisans who could later claim legitimately to have been the liberators of their native countries.

Of the two states which hosted the most active guerrilla movements of the war, only in Yugoslavia did a partisan leader emerge who was to prove an able statesman as well as an efficient military commander. Josip Broz—Tito was his best-known alias among the several he used in the underground—won over supporters who had originally aided his enemies, gained a clear military victory over German occupying forces, established a national Communism which repudiated Soviet control in the Cold War, and held together mutually disparate and hostile nationalities during his lifetime. The significance of that achievement became apparent after civil wars tore apart Yugoslavia in the 1990s.

In 1939 Yugoslavia had an area of 99,000 square miles—about the same size as Great Britain. Nine-tenths of that area was dominated by a wild and beautiful complex of rugged mountains. Within these mountains were narrow river valleys that provided some fertile soil. Along the coast facing Italy was a dense chain of small islands. Although there were some mineral resources, these had never been sufficiently exploited to make Yugoslavia the vital area that Greece became for the German war economy.

Yugoslavia had been established after World War I. Its original component was the monarchical state of Serbia, whose role in the assassination of the Austrian archduke Maximilian had been the *casus belli* of World War I. The Croats, along with Slovenes and Bosnians, had been placed under Serbia's leadership without specific guarantees of a federal relationship. Attached to national differences were religious ones. The Croats and Slovenes were predominantly Roman Catholic. The Serbs and Macedonians belonged to the Eastern Orthodox Church. The Bosnians were Moslems. Rivalry also existed in respect to cultural orientations, with the Croats more attached to western European culture than the Serbs. But the great masses of people were still tied to peasant life, with limited horizons, a difficult existence on poor soil, and blood feuds which took a heavy toll.

Political violence was endemic in the years between the two world wars. The leader of the Croats was shot to death on the floor of the Yugoslav parliament in 1928, and the king, Alexander I, was murdered in Marseilles in 1934 by a Bosnian under Croat direction. Alexander's son, Peter, was too young to assume the throne, and government fell into the hands of his Anglophile uncle, Paul, who became the regent. Yugoslavia might have escaped several years of warfare had not Mussolini set off his ill-fated thrust into Albania and Greece, a move that required a military rescue by Hitler. Even then, Yugoslavia might have been spared conflict if the young king, backed by a coup, had not assumed his duties on March 27, 1941, and reversed Paul's decision to sign the Tripartite Pact with Italy and Germany which had preserved Yugoslavia's neutrality. The consequence of King Peter's action was a full-scale attack by the Germans on April 6, 1941.

The Nazi invasion was attended by the usual severity reserved for Slavic peoples. Hitler regarded Yugoslavia as a "festering sore," and the Luftwaffe bombed Belgrade while the panzers and motorized infantry rolled across Croatia. Yugoslav generals sought surrender on April 14, but the monarch and members of his government and military fled to Cairo and then to Britain, forming another of the exile governments crowding London. Germany's allies took their share of the spoils: the Italians occupied Montenegro, part of Dalmatia, Kosovo, western Macedonia, and part of Slovenia; the Bulgarians occupied most of Montenegro; and Hungary took a portion of Vojvodina and Croatia.

Serbia became a new state under the puppet General Milan Nedić and received the most direct German supervision. A native Serbian fascist movement also flowered, complete with a military organization called the Serbian Volunteer Corps. Meanwhile, Croatia was constituted by the Germans as an independent state, including within its borders Bosnia and part of Dalmatia. This state was left to Italian supervision. Mussolini recognized the leadership of Ante Pavelić, who led a vicious fascist movement called the *Ustashi*. Pavelić instituted a program by which the million-and-a-half Serbs within Croatia were either expelled or forced to convert to the Roman Catholic church. The pogroms against the Orthodox Serbs took the lives of from 600,000 to 900,000 men, women, and children. Some were shot; some were knifed; some were beaten with clubs; and the bodies of the dead were thrown into ravines. Bosnian Moslems were also killed en masse by the *Ustashi*. Both they and the Jews could not easily avail themselves of the only means of escaping the terror—conversion to Roman Catholicism.

The German-sponsored brutality of these early days brought joint opposition from the two best-known resistance leaders and their supporters. The Chetniks (the term derived from *cheta*, armed band) led by Colonel Draža Mihailović were predominantly Serbs. Beginning as a small nucleus of Serbian officers, they had fled from the German troops and gained support for their guerrilla activities both from the Yugoslav government in exile and from British intelligence forces. The Croatian resistance forces, the Partisans, were led by Tito, who had been a leader of a Communist movement before the war. In the early days Mihailović and Tito both engaged in action against the Germans and the *Ustashi*.

By the fall of 1941, however, the Germans had established their customary pattern of retribution against resistance movements. Late in October 1941 a German column on the way back to their base was ambushed by Partisans, and a dozen soldiers were killed, thirty wounded. In response the Germans blocked all exits from the town of Kragujevac, rounded up its 7,000 males, divided them into groups of forty and machine-gunned each batch until only 600 were left alive to serve as hostages against new Partisan strikes. To dissuade further Partisan action, German authorities promised to kill 100 civilians for each German soldier slain.

This event marked the beginning of a lengthy period during which Mihailović and the Chetniks preferred to play a waiting game until significant outside aid could be obtained. At the same time they began to show hostility toward Tito's Partisans, whose minor successes, they believed, were not worth the heavy toll of lives taken by the Germans in reprisals. But the British and Americans, who had supported Mihailović, began increasingly to feel that the Chetnik leader was much more interested in killing Partisans than in killing Germans. It must be added, however, that the British support appears to have been rather marginal in terms of arms and munitions. From first to last, provision from the air was difficult since landing strips were frequently nonexistent. Materiel had to be brought in at night to places marked by lighted fires while fending off German fighters actively seeking to destroy slow-moving British supply aircraft.

During the year 1942 British military missions in Yugoslavia began to report consistently that Mihailović was doing little to fight the Germans. In contrast the Partisans of Tito were active and determined. This activity had, of course, been encouraged by the entry of the Soviet Union into the war. Tito had spent many years in the Soviet Union and had preserved his connection with the Comintern. Some followers who rallied to his leadership were peasants motivated by the basic hope that in the postwar era they could acquire land from those who owned it. Others were aware that the proximity of Soviet territory to the Balkans offered a hope of direct military assistance that could not be expected from Great Britain.

By the early part of 1943 British leaders were convinced that the prosecution of the war in the Balkans could best be achieved by switching support from Mihailović to Tito. The most significant liaison with Tito and the major source of information on Partisan activity was Brigadier Fitzroy Maclean, who parachuted into Yugoslavia on September 17, 1943. Maclean found

Tito a self-possessed leader who inspired the confidence of his followers in his decisions. Through the period that followed, substantial military aid from both the British and the Americans came to Tito. Maclean detailed in his accountings the life of the Partisans: always on the move, women joining men in the fighting, both men and women often carrying strings of hand grenades draped about their persons. As they moved from one point of fighting to another, the Partisans carried their wounded with them rather than leaving them to the vengeance of the Germans.

The Partisan cause was aided after the fall of Mussolini by the capture of Italian arms left behind as troops withdrew from islands along the Dalmatian coastline. Still, the Partisan struggle for victory was hard and costly. In the end Soviet forces aided in the capture of Belgrade, but Tito earned the primary position in the postwar government. A temporary arrangement was made with representatives of the former monarch, but it was clear that this compromise would not last.

The patchwork quilt of contending nationalities had not been altered by the war. In the early postwar period Tito imposed a stronger sense of unity but then relied on federal arrangements. The flareup of existing conflicts in Yugoslavia after Communism's collapse has revealed that the vicious internecine warfare of World War II had only been held in check by Tito and his Communist party. Perhaps it may be many more years before the Balkans experience real peace and quiet.

Confused as the story of wartime Yugoslavia was, that of Greece was even more so. Before World War II Greece had already become a dictatorship. The great republican leader, Eleutherios Venizelos, had led Greece into World War I. His differences with King Constantine I in 1923 led to Constantine's abdication and replacement by George II. But an attempted coup in 1924 led Venizelos to abolish the monarchy. Political instability, tied strongly to the Greek military, continued.

In 1935 King George II returned to the throne with promises of constitutional government. Instead he pledged his support to General Ioannis Metaxas, who established a dictatorship. Metaxas, who had studied in the German War College in Berlin, was extremely conservative and monarchist. The regime he established was authoritarian and based on "the spiritual values of God, King, Family, and Country." One of Metaxas's "family" laws was mildly humorous—the length of women's skirts was regulated, and policemen carried rulers to make sure this requirement was obeyed. Robert Ley, the Nazi labor leader, helped organize government controls over workers. Opponents who spoke out against the regime were arrested. Unemployment was reduced, but both taxes and the cost of living rose. Education was made to serve propaganda—references to liberty in Shakespeare's works and in Greek literature were excised. Metaxas considered his regime to be similar to that of Salazar's in Portugal, since both exercised dictatorial controls with the support of the church.

The British were not troubled by the Metaxas regime. They believed the king tried to moderate its severity. Actually the king was never really concerned with popular support. Although the authoritarian nature of the state made it better able to deal with Italy's invasion in 1940, the regime did not seek to mobilize the support of the masses. It was somehow fitting that the minister of the interior had a picture of Adolf Hitler on the wall behind his desk. Both Communists and liberal non-Communist leaders opposed the regime and the king who sponsored it.

Contrary to common assumptions, Hitler knew about Mussolini's plans for an attack on Greece, and German opposition resulted in several delays before Italian forces invaded Greece on October 28, 1940. But the Germans were shocked at the ignoble outcome of their ally's action, since Italian forces were pushed back into Albania. They also received reports that considerably exaggerated the strength of British forces preparing to aid the Greeks. It was thought that British bases in Greece could bring the Rumanian oil fields, on which the Germans were very dependent in this period, under air attack. Greece also had significant deposits of chrome, bauxite, manganese, molybdenum, and nickel and was for the Germans a vital transport area for oil and vital minerals. The Germans also feared the creation of a Turkish-Greek understanding that might strangle the delivery of these resources.

On March 17, 1941, Hitler approved Operation Marita, and German troops invaded Greece from Bulgaria. There had been some British military aid to Greece in anticipation of this action, but the Greeks had rejected the idea of allowing a large body of British troops to enter the country for fear of provoking a German response.

Greek military opposition was minimal—the country was quickly confronted with 75,000 German troops with armor and air support. By April 17 the Greek army was ready to capitulate. Under British pressure, King George II opposed capitulation, and Greece remained technically at war with Germany until April 22, although General Georgios Tsolakoglou had mutinied and signed an armistice two days earlier.

The Germans gave a section of Greece to the Bulgarians and another to the Italians but retained for themselves the key central parts and several Aegean islands. General Tsolakoglou became the first quisling premier. Disaster quickly followed the German occupation. The Bulgarian zone of occupation had produced a sizeable portion of Greece's wheat, rye, and eggs before the war, and this food was now unavailable. Occupying armies closed the only munitions plant in Greece and sent the materiel to Germany. The entire tobacco crop was seized, the Greek merchant marine was purchased at half of its value, and most businesses were taken over at minimal cost. Thus the Greeks had no means of purchasing food supplies abroad. The Germans added to this indignity by assessing heavy occupation costs.

Inflation and famine followed. The price of an oka (2.82 lbs.) of bread rose from 10 drachmas in 1941 to 7,000 in 1942, 13,000 in 1943, and eventually in 1944 to 34 million drachmas. Cheese and other products followed this catastrophic course. By the fall of 1941 acute famine stalked the streets of Greek cities; over 63,000 deaths were recorded in 1941–42. The Greek population, mildly opposed to German occupation at the outset, were bitterly hostile by 1943. The Germans had provided some minimal aid in 1941 but blamed the Italians for not doing more.

The British were aware of the problem confronting their former ally, but were afraid the Germans would simply confiscate food supplies if they were sent. Relief was finally organized in February 1942 by the Swedish government, which managed to ship enough food to prevent massive starvation. The cost was originally assumed by the Greek government in exile, but the sum soon became too large for its resources. The relief expenses were taken over by the United States on January 1, 1943.

Signs of Greek resistance to the German occupation came with the failure of voluntary labor recruitment by the Germans (who said it would help unemployment). Miners were reluctant to serve the Germans, and an early rise in the production of chrome in 1942 was lost in the years which followed. Partisan groups targeted the bauxite and nickel mines for sabotage, and production declined rapidly during the occupation.

Meanwhile, General Tsolakoglou assumed the title of Minister President and was joined by other Metaxas generals. This government made no real effort to moderate German controls. A small Greek fascist party, which talked of Greece having been destroyed by "Anglo-Jewish propaganda," made little headway in winning popular support. A second pro-Nazi government was set up in 1942, and on April 6, 1943, a third prime minister, Ioannis Rallis, was put in office. Rallis had been a deputy leader under Metaxas. The Germans approved. Rallis, they announced, was "a courageous and hard fighter against communism." But by this time the Germans had been defeated in Africa and their position in Greece became more tenuous. Occupying forces in Greece rose to 275,000, and Bulgarian military aid was also increased. The Germans also absorbed the Italian troops in Greece after Mussolini's fall; a number of them were disarmed, while others were sent to Russia. The first Greek Jews who had not starved in the famine or from hard forced labor began the long ride to the death camps on February 13, 1943, and by August some 46,000 Jews from Salonica, their most populous dwelling place, had been sent to Auschwitz. Of Greece's 73,000 Jews, fewer than 10,000 survived.

Greek partisan resistance had early divided itself into two groups. One, led by Colonel Napoleon Zervas, adopted the name National Republican Greek League, commonly abbreviated to the acronym EDES. The rival agency, actually two groups, the National Liberation Front (EAM) and the Greek Popular Liberation Army (ELAS), was called in popular parlance EAM/ELAS. Neither group represented the exiled king, who told his military followers not to get involved.

The role of these two resistance groups was the most controversial issue of the period of German occupation. Zervas, although originally a republican, announced that he had become a monarchist on March 9, 1943 and later led EDES in a civil war with EAM/ELAS after October, 1943. He also made some conciliatory approaches to the Germans. EAM/ELAS was clearly more belligerent toward the Germans, but its wartime leader, Georgios Siantos, never captured popular Greek imagination as Tito had in Yugoslavia.

British policy in the midst of Greek partisan division was never clear and direct. Some British intelligence sources disputed whether EAM/ELAS was dominated by the Communists. Nevertheless the British were able to coordinate the rival elements of both resistance groups for a spectacular raid, destroying the Gorgopotamus railroad bridge on November 25, 1942, and cutting off the flow of German war supplies to North Africa for over four weeks. Although the resistance movements never equalled the dramatic exploits of Tito, the partisans held down 346,000 German troops which might otherwise have been transferred to resist the Allied invasion of France.

Neither the Communist nor non-Communist resistance was fully unified. The only Greek figure with some of Tito's popularity was Athanasios Klaras, who went by the code name Aris Velouchiotis. But his popularity was restricted to his own followers, and he never gained the broad support Tito enjoyed in Yugoslavia. Nevertheless, the overall strength of ELAS was much greater than that of EDES and the latter, poorly directed by its leader, Napoleon Zervas, was destroyed as a fighting force in December, 1944. ELAS forces moved into Athens and threatened to take over the city and dominate a new government. At that point the British confronted a major crisis in their relations with the Greeks.

The British were committed to the support of the return of King George II but they recognized his continued unpopularity. They, particularly Winston Churchill and his supporters, regarded the future of Greece as of vital importance to British security in the Mediterranean. As a consequence, in spite of doubts of the wisdom of his action on the part of liberal-minded groups at home and in the United States, Churchill ordered the intervention of British troops in Athens and the surrounding area against EAM/ELAS. In a civil war in which considerable British forces were employed, ELAS was defeated and many of its combat forces were taken prisoner by the British.

Meanwhile, the king had been pushed to accept a new prime minister, Georgios Papandreou, who had been a follower of the republican Venizelos. Papandreou took his position under the assumption that the king had agreed not to return to Greece until a popular plebiscite had approved the restoration of the monarchy. Arguments still continued until a supposed compromise was reached with a regency to be established under Archbishop Damaskinos and a representative government to be set up. On January 3, 1945, a government of national unity was formed under the popular and non-royalist General Nikolaos Plastieras, but ELAS members continued to be arrested and imprisoned. Liberal British and American voices continued to criticize the British actions. The British sponsorship of an unwanted monarch and their direct intervention in the Greek civil war preserved the divisions and lack of idealism that had always been a weakness of Greek politics.

But as the cold war developed Greece received massive economic aid from the United States, and economic conditions improved although liberal democratic government was never achieved. The tidal wave of cruelty which accompanied the establishment of Communist control in Bulgaria, Albania, and Rumania indicated that a Communist victory in Greece would not have been unattended by harshness and terror. For too many states the horror of Nazi domination was followed by the similar horror of Communist control. The common people who simply wanted peace, a measure of social justice, and the freedom to determine their own fate were to wait half a century before their hopes were even partially realized.

POSTSCRIPT

Those who experienced World War II are rapidly passing from the scene. Soon the public's perception of the war will be fashioned only by the romanticized movie scenes played by actors who were not participants in the actual fighting. Historians, too, tend to forget the real face of war. It has always been too easy for them to gather their understanding of past wars from the viewpoints of the generals who stood removed from the scenes of carnage and suffering.

War is cruel, demeaning, and brutalizing. The ideals which accompany entry into wars become darkened by the elemental quest for personal survival. The average soldier loses the ties which bind him to civilized society. His enemy becomes a thing, not a person. To survive he must shoot his enemies or blow them to bits with artillery fire or roast them in the hell occasioned by flame throwers. If he survives, he may win a Congressional Medal of Honor for heroic action or a Purple Heart for suffering battle wounds. But he must also believe that he is fighting for a goal, a purpose, an ideal. Most often that goal can only be vaguely articulated as the quest for the preservation of his country and its ideals.

The German soldier fought to create a new world order for a master race. But during the conflict (in the Soviet Union especially, but generally everywhere), his ideals gave way to a basic quest to keep on living. To preserve control in occupied territories, German soldiers often shot men, women, and children to create fear in the hearts of their subjects. And for their part, these soldiers could not help but sense the hatred around them as they walked the streets of hostile cities. They knew that a passer-by might turn to toss a hand grenade or that a rifle bullet from a nearby window might take a life.

Those under the heel of the conqueror had already been humiliated by their country's defeat. Everywhere they felt a sense of helplessness. Brave acts of defiance often brought only more deaths. The killing of a German soldier necessarily brought the death of fifty or sometimes a hundred of their countrymen as punishment. Resistance movements were the work of miniscule minorities; they were often not popular since they frequently invited more pointless deaths. Perhaps in retrospect the deeds of some quislings merit less condemnation than they received at the end of the war. Leaders within the occupied countries did not have the freedom of choice nor the luxury of bravado that the governments in exile enjoyed.

Civilians perished in large numbers during the war. Hundreds of thousands of Russians died during the German invasion or in the hell of the work camps established in Germany. The Jewish holocaust claimed six million lives. The Poles lost thousands in the fighting with Germans and Russians and in the forced labor camps. Elsewhere civilians became sacrificial victims of the escalating technology of warfare. Thousands of British subjects died in the German bombings of Britain, just as thousands of Germans died in the increasingly destructive bombing of German cities. Russian forces exacted their vengeance upon retreating German civilians and established sinister regimes in eastern Europe.

For Americans World War II was the last war in which clear ideals were delineated in a worldwide struggle against cruel aggressors. But for many Europeans even today, the legacy of their nation's participation in that war presents both highlights and shadows. Now they can believe their citizens did what they felt they had to do under the existing circumstances. Civilian heroes were in short supply, and their deeds have been celebrated more in retrospect than they were at the time. The occupied nations survived, restored their industries, and recovered their national ideals. Germany and Italy were in turn occupied, demilitarized, and forced to repudiate their wartime deeds. Both are now working for the ideal of a united Europe. Yet national divisions have increased in recent years, and the elemental passions of ethnic hatred have not declined. The great powers have renounced war, but lesser ones have embraced it. It appears that the great wars have been succeeded by minor ones. Civilian pain and suffering is thereby more localized, but it is no less acute. Worst of all, in the long run it may be even more difficult to bring these minor wars to an end than it was to end the great ones.

BIBLIOGRAPHICAL ESSAY

It is surprising to note the paucity of first-person accounts concerning the experiences of those who remained on the European "home front" during World War II (Great Britain excepted). Some of this is due to the difficulty of locating and making use of accounts written in less commonly spoken languages. It seems that there is a legitimate need for more information on this subject, one that has been often bypassed in the innumerable accounts of battles and campaigns. In the essay below I have sought to emphasize those sources which do recount civilian experiences.

GENERAL

The best general histories of World War II are the revised edition of an older book by Peter Calvocoressi, Guy Wint, and John Pritchard, *Total War: Causes and Courses of the Second World War* (New York, 1989) and a newer volume confined to the European scene by M. K. Dziewanowski, *War at Any Price: World War II in Europe, 1939–1945* (Englewood Cliffs, N.J. 1987). The latter is the best and most up-to-date treatment of the war in Europe. Both of these volumes contain considerable coverage of the home fronts. Other general histories of value are Martha Boyd Hoyle, *A World in Flames: A History of World War II* (New York, 1970); David Irving, *Hitler's War* (London, 1977); B. H. Liddell Hart, *History of the Second World War* (New York, 1970); Louis L. Snyder, *The War: A Concise History, 1939–1945* (New York, 1960); James L. Stokesbury, *A Short History of World War II* (New York, 1980); Chester Wilmot, *The Struggle for Europe* (London, 1952); and Gordon Wright, *The Ordeal of Total War* (New York, 1965). A recent study of the workings of the wartime leadership is Alan Wilt, *War from the Top: German and British Military Decision Making during World War II* (Bloomington, Indiana, 1990).

GREAT BRITAIN

The best accounts of the British home front are those of Angus Calder, *The People's War: Britain, 1939–1945* (New York: 1969); Jonathan Croall, *Don't You Know There's A War On? The People's Voice, 1939–1945* (London, 1988); and Peter Lewis, *A People's War* (London, 1986). Other works providing some views of domestic life are Richard Hough and Denis Richards, *The Battle of Britain: The Greatest Air Battle of World War II* (New York, 1989); Liddell Hart's *History of the Second World War* noted previously; and A. J. P. Taylor's *English History, 1914–1945* (New York, 1965). No view of England during World War II would be complete without a reading of Winston Churchill's masterful history, *The Second World War*, 6 vols. (Boston, 1948–1951). Although Churchill's view of the war is one "from the top," his story carries with it the spirit of British resistance.

The story of Britain's interest in science and its effect on technology is found in R. V. Jones, *The Wizard War: British Scientific Intelligence, 1939–1945* (New York, 1978). A recent work seeks to show the atmosphere of anti-Semitism in wartime Britain; it is Tony Kushner, *The Persistence of Prejudice: Antisemitism in British Society during the Second World War* (New York, 1989). First-person accounts worth consulting are Dorothy Sheridan, ed., *Among You Taking Notes . . . the Wartime Diary of Naomi Mitchison, 1939–1943* (London, 1985); Jan Struther, et al., *Women of Britain: Letters from England* (New York, 1941) features a running commentary by Beatrice Curtis Brown.

SOVIET UNION

The recent work by John Barber and Mark Harrison, *The Soviet Home Front, 1941–1945: A Social and Economic History of the USSR in World War II* (New York, 1991) has provided an in-depth view of domestic affairs in the Soviet Union that was not previously available. It is, however, based largely on government records, and the personal views of participants are still lacking. As a consequence some of the older studies are still of considerable value for the story of the Russian struggle in World War II. Among the most valuable are a volume in Time-Life Books' history of World War II by Nicholas Bethell, *Russia Besieged* (Alexandria, Va., 1977); Alan Clark, *Barbarossa: The Russian-German Conflict, 1941–45* (New York, 1965); Alex de Jonge, *Stalin and the Shaping of the Soviet Union*, (New York, 1986); Ilya Ehrenburg, *The War: 1941–1945*. Vol. V of Men, Years—Life (Cleveland and New York, 1964); George Fischer, *Soviet Opposition to Stalin* (Cambridge, Mass., 1952); Nikita Khrushchev, *Krushchev Remembers* (Boston, 1970); Alexander Werth, *Russia at War, 1941–1945* (New York, 1964); and Earl F. Ziemke, *The Soviet Juggernaut* (Alexandria, Va., 1980).

Particular views of the German campaign and its arousal of partisan reaction are found in the following works: General Wladyslaw Anders, *Hitler's Defeat in Russia* (Chicago, 1953); John Armstrong, ed., *The Soviet Partisans in World War II* (Madison, Wisc. 1964); Omer Bartow, *Hitler's Army: Soldiers, Nazis, and War in the Third Reich* (New York, 1991), narrates the saga of German armies as they fought deep in the Soviet Union and emphasizes the savagery and ferocity of that conflict; see also Alexander Dallin, *German Rule in Russia, 1941–1945* (New York, 1957); Robert Conquest, *The Nation Killers: Soviet Deportation of Nationalities* (New York, 1970). The best treatment of the action of the Soviet partisans is found in Matthew Cooper, *The Phantom War: The German Struggle against Soviet Partisans, 1941–1944* (London, 1979).

Several German soldiers wrote memoirs of their experience in the Soviet Union that may be fleshed out by Soviet accounts in the near future: Helmut Pabst, *The Outermost Frontier: A German Soldier in the Russian Campaign* (London, 1952); and Guy Sajer, *The Forgotten Soldier* (New York, 1972). Parts of Aleksandr I. Solzhenitsyn's *The Gulag Archipelago* (New York, 1974) relate to the Second World War.

FRANCE

In spite of the volume of material on France during World War II, there is still no single work in English that gathers up all the threads and puts them together in a comprehensive account. The major German account of France during the occupation period meets this objective: Eberhard Jäckel, *Frankreich in Hitlers*

Europa. Die deutsche Frankreichpolitik im 2. Weltkrieg (Stuttgart, 1966). The remainder of this bibliographical list is divided into books dealing with France as a whole and those centering specifically on the Vichy regime.

Among the views of the defeat of France are the following: Jacques Benoist-Mechin, *Sixty Days that Shook the West: The Fall of France, 1940* (New York, 1963), which erroneously tries to lay the blame on every country but France; William L. Shirer, *The Collapse of the Third Republic: An Inquiry into the Fall of France in 1940* (New York, 1969), which remains the best account of the military and political aspects of the French defeat.

The literature on France under occupation and the Vichy regime is extensive. The best work, by far, on the French resistance movement is David Schoenbrun, *Soldiers of the Night: The Story of the French Resistance* (New York, 1980). A recent work by Arthur Funk studies the activities of one particular resistance effort in southern France: *Hidden Ally: the French Resistance, Special Operations, and the Landings in Southern France, 1944* (Westport, Conn., 1992). Other studies of value are Russell Miller, *The Resistance* (Alexandria, Va., 1979), and Margaret L. Rossiter, *Women in the Resistance* (New York, 1986). A particular study on Paris during the occupation with excellent illustrations is Henri Michel, *Paris Allemand* (Paris, 1981). See also the work by Lucien Steinberg, *Les Allemands en France, 1940–1944* (Paris, 1980). A more specialized treatment of the French resistance is presented in Max Hastings, *Das Reich: Resistance and the March of the 2nd SS Panzer Division through France, June 1944* (London, 1981). Hastings outlines how the French Resistance delayed the movement of a powerful German armored division that might otherwise have jeopardized the Allied landing in Normandy.

The literature on Vichy and the problems of French collaboration with the Germans is most extensive. Probably the best work is John F. Sweets, *Choices in Vichy France: The French Under Nazi Occupation* (New York, 1986). Other studies of this sticky subject are those by Milton Dank, *The French against the French: Collaboration and Resistance* (London, 1978); Paul Farmer, *Vichy: Political Dilemma* (New York, 1955); Bertram M. Gordon, *Collaborationism in France during the Second World War* (Ithica, N.Y., 1980); and Harry Roderick Kedward, *Occupied France: Collabo-*

ration and Resistance, 1940–1944 (New York, 1985). An unusual study of the dilemmas of Vichy is the script, translated from the French, of the famous movie which articulated the tragedy of those years: Marcel Ophuls, *The Sorrow and the Pity: A Film by Marcel Ophuls*, introduction by Stanley Hoffmann (New York, 1972). Henry Rousso has dealt with this problem in more scholarly fashion in his book, *The Vichy Syndrome: History and Memory in France since 1944* (Cambridge, Mass., 1991). Several writers have tied the wartime history of Vichy to the events surrounding the Vilde affair: Martin Blumenson, *The Vilde Affair: Beginnings of the French Resistance* (Boston, 1977); see as well Ladislas de Hoyos, *Klaus Barbie*, tr. Nicholas Courtin (London, 1985); Ted Morgan, *An Uncertain Hour: The French, the Germans, the Jews, the Klaus Barbie Trial, and the City of Lyon, 1940–1945* (New York, 1990) Erna Paris, *Unhealed Wounds: France and the Klaus Barbie Affair* (New York, 1986).

The best study of de Gaulle's role in World War II is that by Arthur L. Funk, *Charles de Gaulle: the Crucial Years, 1943–1945* (Norman, Okla., 1959). A critical biography of de Gaulle is that by Alexander Werth, *De Gaulle: A Political Biography* (New York, 1966). A negative appraisal of de Gaulle's wartime leadership is presented by a French officer who served in London during the war: Robert Mengin, *No Laurels for de Gaulle*, tr. Jay Allen (New York, 1966). The wartime differences between de Gaulle and Roosevelt are considered by Milton Viorst, *Hostile Allies: FDR and Charles de Gaulle* (New York, 1965). Another French view of the end of the war is that by A. J. Liebling, *The Road Back to Paris* (New York, 1988).

GERMANY

How can I avoid mentioning my own work first! It is one of several which explore the feelings of the Germans at home as the war progressed and it became clear that their country would be defeated. Earl R. Beck, *Under the Bombs: The German Home Front, 1942–1945* (Lexington, Ky., 1986). An earlier study is that of Marlis G. Steinert, *Hitler's War and the Germans: Public Mood and Attitude During the Second World War* (Athens, Ohio, 1977). Several studies of Nazi propaganda document the efforts of the regime to preserve morale. The best study is that of Jay W. Baird, *The Mythical World of Nazi War Propaganda* (Minneapolis, 1974); consult also Robert E. Herzstein, *The War that Hitler Won: The Most Infamous Propaganda Campaign in History* (New York, 1978). A German account of the homefront is that by Wolfgang Paul, *Der Heimatkrieg, 1939 bis 1945* (Esslingen-am-Neckar, 1980). A whole series of studies dealing with the effects of the bombings in Germany has been published in recent years, among them Heinz Bardua, *Stuttgart im Luftkrieg, 1939–1945*, in *Veröffentlichungen des Archivs der Stadt Stuttgart*, vol. 23. (Stuttgart, 1967); Martin Broszat, Elke Fröhlich, and Falk Wiesemann, eds., *Bayern in der NS-Zeit*, vol. 1, *Soziale Lage und politisches Verhalten der Bevölkerung im Spiegel vertraulicher Berichte* (München, 1977): Martin Broszat, Elke Fröhlich, and Anton Grossmann, eds. *Bayern in der NS-Zeit*, vol. 3, *Herrschaft und Gesellschaft im Konflikt*, Part B (München, 1981); *Bayern in der NS-Zeit*, vol. 4, *Herrschaft und Gesellschaft im Konflikt*, Part C (München, 1981); Hans-Georg Kraume, *Duisburg im Krieg, 1939–1945* (Düsseldorf, 1982); Hans Rumpf, *Das war der Bombenkrieg. Deutsche Städte im Feuersturm. Ein Dokumentärbericht* (Oldenburg-Hamburg, 1961); Alan S. Milward, *Die deutsche Kriegswirtschaft, 1933–1945*, in *Vierteljahrshefte für Zeitgeschichte*, no. 12 (Stuttgart, 1966). All of these books, as well as the studies in English, have been overtaken by the massive work of Olaf Groehler, *Bombenkrieg gegen Deutschland* (Berlin, 1990) which recognizes that urban bombing was a strategy begun by the Germans but underscores the belief that the British should have adopted much earlier a more strategic approach—the targeting of synthetic oil resources and transportation.

Aspects of the bombing war from the Allied side are found in Fred Majdalany, *The Fall of Fortress Europe* (Garden City, N.Y., 1968); Martin Middlebrook, *The Battle of Hamburg: Allied Bomber Forces Against a German City in 1943* (London, 1980); Alfred C. Mierzejewski, *The Collapse of the German War Economy, 1944–1945: Allied Air Power and the German National Railway* (Chapel Hill, 1988). Mierzejewski proves that the destruction of the German transportation system at the end of the war did contribute significantly to the German defeat. See also Gordon

Musgrove, *Operation Gomorrah: The Hamburg Firestorm Raids* (London, 1981); and R. J. Overy, *The Air War, 1939–1945* (London, 1980).

Accounts of the Nazi regime during the latter days of the war are found in a number of works. The author believes that the general history of the Nazi state by Karl Dietrich Bracher, *The German Dictatorship: The Origins, Structure, and Effects of National Socialism* (New York, 1970) has not and is not likely to be bettered by new research. Other works of significance are as follows: the most readable biography of Hitler is that by John Toland, *Adolf Hitler*, 2 vols. (New York, 1976). See also Joachim Fest, *Hitler* (New York, 1974); Richard Grunberger, *A Social History of the Third Reich* (London, 1971); Heinz Höhne, *The Order of the Death's Head: the Story of Hitler's S.S.* (New York, 1971); Edward L. Homze, *Foreign Labor in Nazi Germany* (Princeton, 1971); Robert L. Koehl, *RKFDV: German Resettlement and Population Policy, 1939–1945* (Cambridge, 1957). The volume by Jochen von Lang, *Bormann: the Man who Manipulated Hitler* (London, 1979), provides sharp pictures of the end of the Nazi regime. So also do the volumes by Albert Speer, *Inside the Third Reich: Memoirs* (New York, 1970) and by Marlis Steinert, *23 Days: The Final Collapse of Nazi Germany* (New York, 1969). A recent study by Charles Duffy, *Red Storm on the Reich: The Soviet March on Germany, 1945* (New York, 1991) provides in English details of the harshness of the Russian advance into Germany; cf. Jürgen Thorwald, *Die grosse Flucht. Es begann an der Wechsel, das Ende an der Elbe* (Rev. ed., Stuttgart, 1968).

New information and conclusions about the role of women in wartime Germany is presented by Leila J. Rupp, *Mobilizing Women for War: German and American Propaganda, 1939–1945* (Princeton, 1978).

Although general treatments of the Holocaust are presented later in this essay, particular materials relating the Final Solution to wartime developments within Germany are found in Sarah Gordon, *Hitler, Germans, and the "Jewish Question"* (Princeton, 1984). See also Leonard Gross, *The Last Jews in Berlin* (New York, 1982).

The German resistance to Hitler has been considered in a number of works. Among them, the most readable and valuable are Richard Hanser, *A Noble Treason. The Revolt of the Munich Students against Hitler* (New York, 1979); Terence Prittie, *Germans against Hitler* (Boston, 1964); Ger von Roon, *German Resistance to Hitler: Count von Moltke and the Kreisau Circle* (New York, 1971); Hans Rothfels, *The German Opposition to Hitler* (Hinsdale, Ill., 1946); Inge Scholl, *Students against Tyranny: The Resistance of the White Rose, Munich, 1942–43* (Middlebrook, Conn., 1970).

Some readable first-person accounts are available—each, of course, represents only a single view of what occurred, but some of the feeling for life in Nazi Germany may be found: Frances Henry, *Victims and Neighbors: A Small Town in Nazi Germany Remembered* (South Hadley, Mass., 1984); Zofka Kruk, *The Taste of Fear: A Polish Childhood in Germany, 1939–1946* (London, 1973); Friedrich Percyval Reck-Malleczewen, *Diary of a Man in Despair* (London, 1970); Elsie Wendel, *Hausfrau at War: A German Woman's Account of Life in Hitler's Reich* (London, 1957); Mathilde Wolff-Mönckeberg, *On the Other Side: To My Children, from Germany, 1940–1945* (London, 1979).

ITALY

The books in English on the Italian home front are few. Far and away the most important source for the subject is the study by Charles F. Delzell, *Mussolini's Enemies: The Italian Anti-Fascist Resistance* (Princeton, 1961). Other English-language sources are the studies of the role of women under Fascism and their part in the resistance by Victoria De Grazia, *The Culture of Consent* (Cambridge, 1981) and *How Fascism Ruled Women: Italy, 1922–1945* (Berkeley, 1992). Other works in English dealing with the Italian resistance are Giovanni Pesce, *And No Quarter: An Italian Partisan in World War II. Memoirs of Giovanni Pesce*, tr. Frederick M. Shaine (Athens, Ohio, 1972); Maria de Blasio Wilhelm, *The Other Italy: Italian Resistance in World War II* (New York, 1988); and David W. Ellwood, *Italy, 1943–1945* (The Politics of Liberation Series) (Bath, UK, 1985). An earlier study still has value: Massimo Salvadori, *A Brief History of the Patriot Movement in Italy, 1943–1945* (Chicago, 1954).

The major studies of Italian Fascism have heavily emphasized the character and role of the dictator. It seems unlikely that they will be surpassed anytime in the near future: F. W. Deakin, *The Brutal Friendship. Mussolini, Hitler and the Fall of Italian Fascism* (New York, 1962); Ivone Kirkpatrick, *Mussolini, A Study in Power* (New York, 1964); Denis Mack Smith, *Italy: A Modern History* (Ann Arbor, Mich., 1959); Christopher Leeds, *Italy under Mussolini* (London, 1972); and Herbert L. Matthews, *The Fruits of Fascism* (New York, 1943), which has particular importance for its study of the Italian economy before the involvement in world war. A recent study of Mussolini's wartime military leadership is MacGregor Knox, *Mussolini Unleashed, 1939–1941. Politics and Strategy in Fascist Italy's Last War* (New York, 1982).

Among the older studies of Fascism still of value are the books by Dante L. Germino, *The Italian Fascist Party in Power* (Minneapolis, 1959); the study by Edward R. Tannenbaum, *The Fascist Experience* (New York, 1972); the revealing diaries of Mussolini's foreign minister, Count Galeazzo Ciano, *Ciano's Diary* (London, 1950); the study of Mussolini's most dislikeable follower by Harry Fornari, *Mussolini's Gadfly: Roberto Farinacci* (Nashville, 1971).

English-language studies that cover the closing stages of Fascism and the consequences of its collapse include the following: Raleigh Trevelyan, *Rome '44: The Battle for the Eternal City* (New York, 1982), which presents an intimate picture of the city and of the military events surrounding it; H. Stuart Hughes, *The United States and Italy* (Cambridge, 1965); Giuseppe Mammarella, *Italy After Fascism: A Political History, 1943–1965* (Notre Dame, 1966); and Maurice F. Neufeld, *Italy: School for Awakening Countries. The Italian Labor Movement in Its Political, Social, and Economic Setting from 1800 to 1960* (Ithaca, N.Y., 1961).

Italian studies of the resistance include the following: Roberto Battaglia, *Storia della Resistenza italiana, 8 settembre 1943–25 aprile 1945* (Torino, 1964); Philip V. Cannistraro, *La fabbrica del consenso: fascismo e mass media* (Bari, 1975); Franco Catalano, *L'Italia dalla dittatura alla democrazia, 1919/1948*, 2 vols. (Milano, 1972); Frederico Chabodi, *L'Italia contemporanea, 1918–1948* (Turin, 1961); Armando Gavagnin, *Vent' anni di resistenza al fascismo* (Turin, 1957); Mario Giovana, *Resistenza e guerra di Liberazione*

(Milano, 1977); Giorgio Pisano, *Storia della guerra civile in Italia, 1943–1945* (Milano, 1965).

POLAND AND THE JEWISH HOLOCAUST

The literature on the Holocaust grows by leaps and bounds. Each new first-person account adds to the overwhelming sense of tragedy. Among the general histories of the Holocaust, those which provide the best overall summation are the following: Yehuda Bauer, *A History of the Holocaust* (New York, 1982); Lucy Dawidowicz, *The War Against the Jews, 1933–1945* (New York, 1975); Raoul Hilberg, *The Destruction of the European Jews* (Chicago, 1967); and Walter Laqueur, *The Terrible Secret: An Investigation into the Suppression of Information about Hitler's "Final Solution"* (London, 1980). The major account of the failure of the United States to try to bomb the concentration camps is David S. Wyman, *The Abandonment of the Jews: America and the Holocaust, 1941–1945* (New York, 1985).

Two books dealing with Polish oppression under Nazi occupation appropriate the term "holocaust." The comparison is debatable since the Polish state *was* resurrected and restored, whereas Jewish communities could never be restored. Still, one must respect the passion of those who wrote on behalf of the Poles, who indeed suffered tremendously under the Nazis: Richard C. Lukas, *The Forgotten Holocaust: The Poles Under German Occupation, 1939–1944* (Lexington, Ky., 1986); and Bogdan Wytwycky, *The Other Holocaust: Many Circles of Hell* (Washington, D.C., 1980). Other studies of Poland during the Second World War are John Courtovidis and Jaime Reynolds, *Poland, 1939–1947* (Leicester, 1986); Jozef Garlinski, *Poland in the Second World War* (Basingstoke, 1985) and *Poland, S.O.E. and the Allies* (London, 1969); Jan Gross, *Polish Society Under the German Occupation: The General Government, 1939–1945* (Princeton, 1979); Stefan Korbonski, *Fighting Warsaw: The Story of the Polish Underground State, 1939–1945* (New York, 1956) and *The Polish Underground State: A Guide to the Underground, 1939–1945* (Boulder, Colo., 1978); Jan Karski, *Story of a Secret State* (Boston, 1944). The major German work on the Polish occupation is that of Martin

Broszat, *Nationalsozialistische Polenpolitik, 1939–1945 (Stuttgart,* 1961).

OTHER HOMEFRONTS

General Studies

Among the major efforts to summarize the resistance in Europe, the following works provide readable accounts: M. R. D. Foot, *Resistance: European Resistance to Nazism, 1940–1945* (London, 1976); Jørgen Haestrup, *Europe Ablaze: An Analysis of the History of the European Resistance Movements, 1939–45.* (Odense, 1978) and *European Resistance Movements, 1939–1945: A Complete History* (Westport, Conn., 1981); and Stephen Hanes and Ralph White, eds., *Resistance in Europe, 1939–1945* (London, 1976). The other side of the coin, the story of collaboration with the Nazis, is provided in J. Lee Ready's *The Forgotten Axis: Germany's Partners and Foreign Volunteers in World War II* (New York: 1987).

Belgium

The story of Belgium during World War II is the most sparsely told of all European states. The only English source the author found was John Gillingham, *Belgian Business in the Nazi New Order.* (Ghent, 1977); one partial account in French is that by Jules Gerard-Libois and José Gotovitch, *L'an 40, la Belgique occupée* (Bruxelles, 1971). A German source provides a more complete coverage: Wilfried Wagner, *Belgien in der deutschen Politik während des Zweiten Weltkrieges,* Wehrwirtschaftliche Forschungen: Abteilung Militärgeschichtliche Studien, 18 (Boppard-am-Rhein, 1974).

Netherlands

The principal study of the occupied Netherlands is that of Werner Warmbrunn, *The Dutch Under German Occupation* (Stanford, Calif., 1963). Two studies underscore the hardships suffered by the Dutch in the last stages of the war: Zena Stein, et al., *Famine and Human Development: the Dutch Hunger Winter of 1944–1945* (New York, 1975); and Henri A. van der Zee, *The Hun-*

ger Winter: Occupied Holland, 1944–5 (London, 1982). The story of Anne Frank is told in her own journal, published as *The Diary of a Young Girl,* tr. B. M. Mooyart (Garden City, N.Y., 1952) and in the account of Ernst Schnabel, *Anne Frank: A Portrait in Courage,* tr. Richard and Clara Winston (New York, 1958); a lesser-known account by another Jewish girl is that of Leesha Rose, *The Tulips are Red* (South Brunswick, N.J., 1978). The only German account of the occupation are the speeches of Artur Seyss-Inquart, *Vier Jahre in den Niederländen. Gesammelte Reden* (Amsterdam, 1944).

Norway

The two major sources for the history of the occupation in Norway are both rather imposing reading: Alan S. Milward, *The Fascist Economy in Norway* (Oxford, 1972), and Richard Petrow, *The Bitter Years: The Invasion and Occupation of Denmark and Norway, April 1940–May 1945* (New York, 1974). A more recent study dealing with all of Scandinavia has significant sections on Norway and Denmark: Henrik S. Nissen, ed., *Scandinavia during the Second World War* (Minneapolis, 1983). Studies of the Norwegian resistance indicate that more of it was sponsored by the British than by local groups: Dorothy Baden-Powell, *Operation Jupiter: SOE's Secret War in Norway* (London, 1982); Bjorne Boye and Trygve M. Agler, *The Fight of the Norwegian Church against Nazism* (New York, 1943); Tore Gjelsvik, *Norwegian Resistance, 1940–1945* (London, 1978). A fascinating account of the destruction of the German heavy water installation in Norway is provided by Thomas Gallagher, *Assault in Norway: Sabotaging the Nazi Nuclear Bomb* (New York, 1975).

Denmark

Denmark's wartime history is the subject of the volumes by Ernst Mentze, *5 Years: The Occupation of Denmark in Pictures* (Malmo, Sweden, 1946) and Richard Petrow, *The Bitter Years: The Invasion and Occupation of Denmark and Norway, April 1940– May 1945 (New York,* 1974). On the Danish resistance see Jørgen Haestrup, *Secret Alliance: A Study of the Danish Resistance Movement, 1940–1945,* 3 vols. (Odense, 1976); see also John O.

Thomas, *The Giant-Killers: The Story of the Danish Resistance Movement, 1940–1945* (New York, 1976).

Yugoslavia

The primary first-person description of Tito and his Partisans is that given by the British brigadier Fitzroy Maclean in his book entitled *Eastern Approaches* (London, 1950). Maclean believed strongly in Tito's leadership and was principally responsible for securing British and American support for him. See also Michael McConville, *A Small War in the Balkans: British Military Involvement in Wartime Yugoslavia, 1944–1945* (London, 1986). The author has not been impressed by the effort of David Martin to defend Mihailovič: *Ally Betrayed: The Uncensored Story of Tito and Mihailovič* (Englewood Cliffs, N.J., 1946). Tito is also the subject of an insider's biography: Vladimir Dedijer, *Tito* (New York, 1953); see also Ahmet Donlagic, Zarlo Atackovic, and Dusan Plenca, *Yugoslavia in the Second World War* (Belgrade, 1967). A scholarly study of the Chetniks is that by Jozo Tomasevich, *War and Revolution in Yugoslavia, 1941–1945: The Chetniks* (Stanford, 1975).

Two views of the German problems in Yugoslavia are found in Paul N. Hehn, *The German Struggle Against Yugoslav Guerrillas in World War II: German Counter-Insurgency in Yugoslavia, 1941–1943* (Boulder, Colo., 1979) and Karl Hnilicka, *Das Ende auf dem Balkan 1944/45. Die militärische Räumung Jugoslaviens durch die deutsche Wehrmacht. (Göttingen, 1979)*.

Greece

Materials relating to Greece are skimpy and not very readable. The best coverage is that of John Lewis Hondras, *Occupation and Resistance: The Greek Agony, 1941–44* (New York, 1983), but the complexity of events and abundance of names make it difficult reading. Less satisfactory is the volume by Charles Cruickshank, *Greece, 1940–1941* (London, 1976).

Czechoslovakia

The tragedy of Czechoslovakia's division during World War II (lamentably repeated in 1993) has received a few scholarly examinations. For the Czech perspective on the story see Vojtech

Mastny, *The Czechs under Nazi Rule: The Failure of National Resistance, 1939–42* (New York, 1971) and S. Harrison Thomson, *Czechoslovakia in European History* (Princeton, N.J. 1953). The contrasting story of the Slovak state is told by Yeshayahu Jelinek, *The Parish Republic: Hlinka's Slovak People's Party, 1939–1945* (New York, 1976).

INDEX